D0554064

The Theatre of P.G. Wodehouse

The Theatre of
P. G. WODEHOUSE

David A. Jasen

B.T. Batsford Ltd   London

by the same author:

A Bibliography and Reader's Guide to
the First Editions of P.G. Wodehouse

P.G. Wodehouse: A Portrait of a Master

The Uncollected Wodehouse

**Frontispiece. In the
beginning: PGW at 21.
Aloof yet attentive to
the human comedy of
errors.**

First published 1979
Copyright David Jasen 1979

Filmset in 'Monophoto' Photina by
Servis Filmsetting Ltd, Manchester
Printed in Great Britain by
The Anchor Press Ltd, Tiptree, Essex
for the Publishers, B.T. Batsford Ltd,
4 Fitzhardinge Street, London W1H 0AH

ISBN 0 7134 1584 3

Contents

Acknowledgments

I am grateful to Raymond Mander and Joe Mitchenson for their kindness in searching out and supplying photographs from their Theatre Collection. Also to the Theatre Collection of the New York Public Library. To Mark Klamkin for helping to photograph the author's personal collection of Wodehousiana. And finally, the author's appreciation to Karen Rydzewski, who assisted editorially.

Introduction

P.G. Wodehouse. That's pronounced 'woodhouse', not 'woadhouse'. The family retained the Old English spelling, and Wodehouse was traditional.

And he was also creative. His articles, books, and theatre kept the world laughing for over 75 years. In that time, Jeeves and Bertie Wooster, Lord Emsworth and, of course, the Empress became household words and certainly classics of contemporary humour. But this creativity came at some expense. Very much like Emsworth, who wished to be left alone with his beloved pig, Wodehouse demanded solitude. A solitude often imposed upon by an overbearing outside world. The kindhearted author would allow these intrusions, but he knew that his real inspiration flourished in seclusion.

Flourished is almost inadequate to describe his literary contributions. If his 97 books are noteworthy, even more impressive are his 285 short stories and a hundred more articles. But the theatre was the foundation of Wodehouse's successful career, and accordingly his musicals number 33 and his straight plays 18. Most important, Wodehouse wrote the lyrics for over 200 songs and formed one-third of the theatrical triumvirate of Bolton, Wodehouse, and Kern, 'the trio of musical fame', the pioneers who developed the American musical comedy.

Wodehouse was born in Guildford, England, on 15 October 1881, and died in Remsenburg, New York, on 14 February 1975. He was a prolific writer, the foremost humorist of the twentieth century. And this is his theatre.

CURTAIN RAISER

'Over the years I have held (PGW) as the model of light verse in the song form.'
HOWARD DIETZ

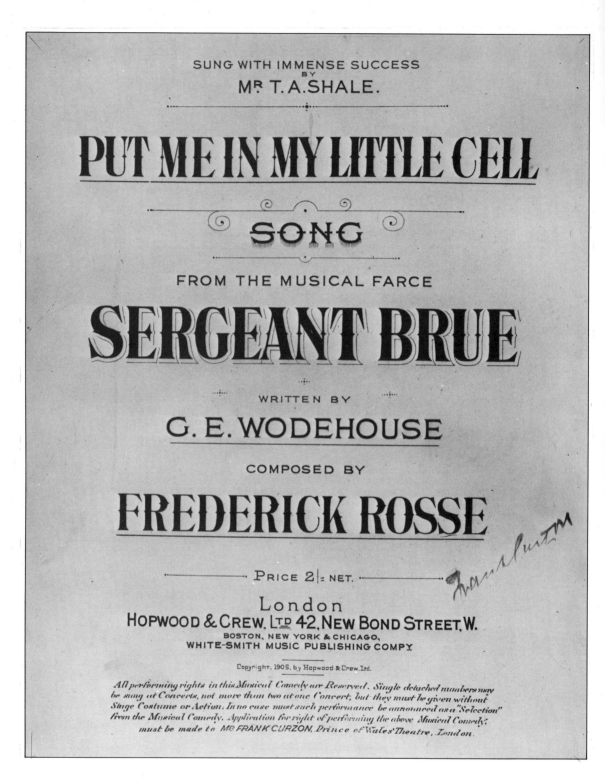

PGW's first taste of theatre, soured slightly by an
initial mistake, occurred when actor-manager Owen
Hall commissioned him to interpolate a lyric for five
guineas.

Sergeant Brue*

10 December 1904 (152 performances)
Strand Theatre, London

Producer: Frank Curzon
Book: Owen Hall
Music: Liza Lehmann
Lyrics: J. Hickory Wood
Scenery: Julian Hicks
Musical Director: Frederick Rosse

Cast in the order of appearance

Sergeant Brue, of the 'C' Division	WILLIE EDOUIN
Michael Brue, his son	FARREN SOUTAR
Aurora Brue, his daughter	ALICE HOLLANDER
Daisy (servant)	JESSICA LAIT
Mabel Widgett	NINA WOOD
Vivienne Russell	NELLIE SEYMOUR
Louise Clair	KITTY ASHMEAD
Eva Graham	DOROTHY DREW
'Arriet	VALERIE DE LACY
Gerald Treherne	ARTHUR APPLEBY
Matthew Habishom, a Solicitor	EDWARD KIPLING
Inspector Gorringe	S. BROOKE
Mr. Lambe	PEET LESLIE
Erskine Murray	HARRY LAMBART
Captain Bay	MICHAEL SANTLEY
Mr. Crank (Magistrate)	FRED LACEBY
Crookie Scrubbs, a criminal	ARTHUR WILLIAMS
Lady Bickenhall	MILLIE LEGARDE

Act I   Michael Brue's hairdressing saloon
Act II   The Green Park Hotel
Act III   Scene 1 – Crawlborough Street Police Court
Scene 2 – 75 Berkeley Square

Published lyric by PGW:
Put Me In My Little Cell

* All cast lists and musical numbers are from opening night programmes.

11

English star Willie Edouin was the sergeant of this police farce.

Sergeant Brue

24 April 1905 (152 performances)
Knickerbocker Theatre, New York

Producer: Charles B. Dillingham
Stage Director: Herbert Gresham
Musical Director: Watty Hydes

Cast

Sergeant Brue, of the 'C' Division	FRANK DANIELS
Michael Brue, his son	ALFRED HICKMAN
Aurora Brue, his daughter	SALLIE FISHER
Daisy, a servant	CLARA BELLE JEROME
Mabel Widgett	CONSTANCE EASTMAN
Vivienne Russell	ELPHIE SNOWDEN
Louise Clair	MARY CLAYTON
Florence Latham	MYRTLE McGRAIN
Nellie Mayne	IRENE CAMERON
Dollie Read	CLAIRE LESLIE
Cissie Raynor	AILEEN GOODWIN
Madge Dawson	DELLA CONNOR
Olive Day	GRETA BURDICK
Gerald Treherne	WALTER PERCIVAL
Matthew Habishom, a lawyer	NACE BONVILLE
Inspector Gorringe	JAMES REANY
Rev. John Lamb (Charity Jim)	LAWRENCE WHEAT
Captain Bay (Radium Jack)	DAVID BENNETT
Percy Procter	GEORGE LESTOCQ
Haddon Wallis	LOUIS FITZROY
Mr. Crank, magistrate	GILBERT CLAYTON
Crookie Scrubbs, a criminal	HARRY MacDONOUGH
Dot, a flower girl	IDA GABRIELLE
Pippins, a newsboy	SALLY DALY
Bill Nokes. a coster	LEAVITT JAMES
Bridget, his wife	LESLIE MAYO
Lady Bickenhall	BLANCHE RING
	(specially engaged)

The Beauty of Bath

'Teddy' Royce began his nine-show association with PGW in this early London production. Son of the famous actor Edward Royce, Teddy was the leading choreographer and director of the twentieth-century musical comedy theatre, both in the West End and on Broadway, and worked for the greatest producers of his age (George Edwardes, Charles Frohman, Charles Dillingham, Florenz Ziegfeld). Royce continued his relationship with Wodehouse productions through the Princess Theatre shows and beyond.

PGW's 'Cell' braided his career with Sir Seymour Hicks. Impressed by Wodehouse's lyrical debut, this actor-manager employed him as a utility lyricist for two pounds a week. Hicks' repertory company had a faithful following, and in these productions Hicks showed his theatrical flair: he always opened the show while his wife Ellaline Terriss was always the last of the cast to make her entrance. Pictured here are Hicks and Terriss in a bus outside their Aldwych Theatre at the time of *Beauty of Bath*.

The Beauty of Bath

19 March 1906 (287 performances)
Aldwych Theatre, London

Producer: Seymour Hicks
Book: Seymour Hicks and Cosmo Hamilton
Music: Herbert E. Haines
Lyrics: Chas. H. Taylor
Scenery: Walter Hann
Dances & Choral Effects: Edward Royce
Stage Director: Edward Royce
Musical Director: Karl Kiefert

Cast in the order of appearance

Lieut. Richard Alington, R.N.	SEYMOUR HICKS	The Countess of Orpington	VERA MORRIS
		The Comtesse Thérèse Rosemere	RENEE DE MONTEL
Viscount Bellingham	WILLIAM LUGG		
Lord Quorn (Betty's cousin)	LAURENCE CAIRD	Lady Delbeck	MARGUERITE LESLIE
		Countess of Chandon	GEORGIE READ
Mr. Beverley (an actor)	STANLEY BRETT	Jane Topit (Betty's maid)	TOPSY SINDEN
Sir Timothy Bun (of Bath)	MURRAY KING	Hot Bun	MAY GATES
Hon. Mortimer Gorst	CECIL KINNAIRD	Iced Bun	LILLIE McINTYRE
Tattersal Spink	BERT SINDEN	Spice Bun	KITTY MELROSE
Hon. Charles Templeton	REGINALD KENNETH	Plum Bun	CLAIRE RICKARDS
The Earl of Orpington	E.W. ROYCE	Rice Bun	HILDA HARRIS
Lemon Goodge (Programme Boy)	MASTER VALCHERA	Crumb Bun	MARION LINDSAY
		Penny Bun	PAULINE FRANCIS
Mrs. Alington (Alington's mother)	ROSINA FILIPPI	Youngest Bun	AGNES HIDGKINSON
		Currant Bun	ENID LESLIE
Hon. Dorothy Quorn (Quorn's sister)	BARBARA DEANE	Cross Bun	MABEL WATSON
		Seed Bun	MABEL ELLIS
Miss Truly St. Cyr (an actress)	MAUDI DARRELL	Home Made Bun	ELSIE KAY
		The Hon. Betty Silverthorne (The Beauty of Bath)	ELLALINE TERRISS
Mrs. Goodge	SYDNEY FAIRBROTHER		
Lady Bun (Sir Timothy's wife)	MOLLIE LOWELL		

Solo Dance in Act II by Topsy Sinden

Act I   The Foyer of the Mascot Theatre, London
           (on a first night)
Act II   The Ball Room at Bellingham House, London
           (next evening)

Left to right: Ellaline Terriss, Barbara Deane, Rosina
Filippi and Stanley Brett.

Ellaline Terriss meets Seymour Hicks.

The Gay Gordons

11 September 1907
Aldwych Theatre, London

Producer: Seymour Hicks
Book: Seymour Hicks
Music: Guy Jones
Lyrics: Arthur Wimperis, C.H. Bovill, P.G. Wodehouse,
   Henry Hamilton
Dances and Choral Effects: Edward Royce

Cast in the order of appearance

Angus Graeme	SEYMOUR HICKS
Nervy Nat	FRED EMNEY
Edmund Siddons	A.W. BASKCOMB
Andrew Quainton	WILLIAM LUGG
John Smith	LAURENCE CAIRD
The Marquis of Dalesbury	CECIL KINNAIRD
Viscount Belstairs	KENNETH MacLAINE
Lord Elmington	ARTHUR ROYD
Lord Meilsham	MERVYN DENE
Archibald Speedy	J.C. BUCKSTONE
Corporal	WILL BISHOP
Janet McCleod	ROSINA FILIPPI
Victoria Siddons	ZENA DARE
Charlotte Siddons	SIDNEY FAIRBROTHER
Mary McCleod	BARBARA DEANE
Lady Millicent Graeme of Lockalt	KATIE BUTLER
Lady Graeme of Lockalt	VERA MORRIS
A Peasant Woman	GEORGINA DELMAR
Peggy Quainton	ELLALINE TERRISS

Act I   A Moor in the Highlands on 'The 12th'
Act II   Tent in the Gardens of Meltrose Castle

Published lyrics in vocal score by PGW:
Now That My Ship's Come Home
You, You, You

Seymour Hicks.

Corker Douglas Fairbanks Sr. effervesced in this, his first leading role, in an adaptation of PGW's novel by the same name.

A Gentleman of Leisure

24 August 1911 (76 performances)
The Playhouse, New York

Producer: William A. Brady
Play: John Stapleton and P.G. Wodehouse (based on PGW's novel)
Director: Edward Elsner

Cast in the order of appearance

Joseph Sutton	EDMUND FORDE
Dana Willets	FRANK KENDRICK
George Fuller	LINDSAY J. HALL
Clarence Macklin	FRANCIS CARLYLE
Sir Spencer Dreever, Bart	ARTHUR LACEBY
Robert Edgar Willoughby Pitt	DOUGLAS FAIRBANKS
'Spike' Mullins	ELMER BOOTH
Lady Blunt	RUTH CHESTER
Sir Thomas Blunt	ROLAND RUSHTON
Mollie Creedon	RUTH SHEPLEY
Phillip Creedon, 'Big Phil'	GEORGE FAWCETT

Act I	Pitt's rooms in Madison Avenue. An evening in June, nearing midnight
Act II	Small drawing room in 'Big Phil's' home, Riverside Drive, after midnight
Act III	The Gables at Sunrise Cove on the Sound. An afternoon, one week later
Act IV	Same as Act I. Three hours later

A Thief for a Night

30 March 1913
McVicker's Theatre, Chicago

McVicker's Annual Spring Production
Beginning Sunday Night, March 30

A THIEF FOR A NIGHT

BY JOHN STAPLETON AND P. G. WODEHOUSE

A Melodramatic Comedy, with

JOHN BARRYMORE

and an unusually good cast, including

ALICE BRADY   FRANK SHERIDAN
ELMER BOOTH   VINCENT STERNROYD
KATE WINGFIELD   ARTHUR LACEBY
GEOFFERY C. STEIN   KATHERINE HARRIS

and many other well known players

SEATS NOW SELLING

EVERY NIGHT AT 8:15
MATINEES WEDNESDAY AND SATURDAY

Rival John Barrymore
was equally refreshing
in a later production,
retitled, and in which
he likewise established
his eminent career.

A son of the D'oyle
Carte Grossmith,
Lawrence commissioned
PGW to adapt this short
story into a showcase
for the former's acting
talents. Lawrence played
an important part in
future Wodehouse
productions.

Brother Alfred

8–19 April 1913 (14 performances)
Savoy Theatre, London

Producer: Lawrence Grossmith
Play: H.W. Westbrook and P.G. Wodehouse (based
  on their short story, 'Rallying Round Old George')

Cast

John Marshall	G. MAYOR-COOKE
Bill Marshall, his son	ARTHUR CHESNEY
George Lattaker	LAWRENCE GROSSMITH
Augustus Arbutt, George's uncle	E.W. GARDEN
Count Fritz von Coslin, Equerry to the Prince	PHILIP CUNNINGHAM
Denman Sturgis, private eye	SYDNEY SKARRATT
Voules, Bill's valet	EDWARD SASS
Sidney	ARTHUR HATHERTON
Mrs. Vanderly	GWYNNETH GALTON
Stella, her daughter	FAITH CELLI
Mamie Foster	MAUD CRESSALL
Pillbeam, Mrs. Vanderly's maid	FLORENCE TEMPEST

The action takes place on Mr. Marshall's S.Y. *Circe*,
anchored off Monte Carlo.
Act I   Late Afternoon. Outside the harbour
Act II   The next morning. In the harbour
Act III   Same as Act II. Evening

Nuts and Wine

4 January 1914 (7 performances)
Empire Theatre, London

Producer: Oscar Barrett, Jr.
Book: C.H. Bovill and P.G. Wodehouse
Music: Frank E. Tours and Melville Gideon
Lyrics: C.H. Bovill, P.G. Wodehouse and Guy Jones
Director: Julian Alfred

Cast
R.G. Knowles
Maidie Hope
Violet Lloyd
Albert Le Fre
Babette
Eric Thorne
Phyllis Bedells
Dorothy Monkman

Act I   Scene 1 – The New Eton
         Scene 2 – The New News
         Scene 3 – The New *Mayflower* Yacht
Act II   Scene 1 – The New Ellis Island
         Scene 2 – The New Little Theatre
         Scene 3 – The New Empire Stores

A tasty and typical Empire theatre entree.

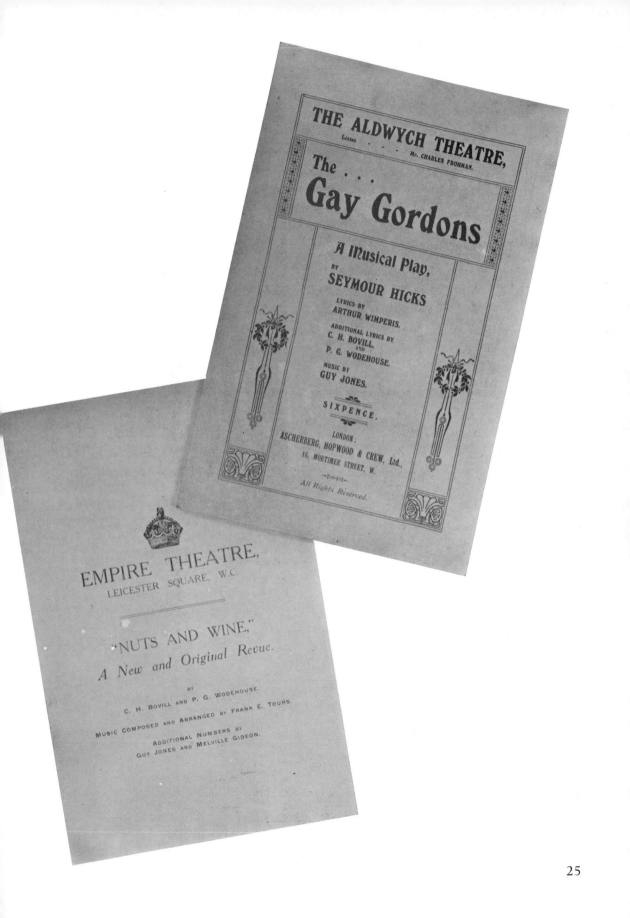

ACT ONE

'Well, Bolton and Wodehouse and Kern have done it again. Every time these three gather together, the Princess Theatre is sold out for months in advance. . . . I like the way they go about a musical comedy. I like the way the action slides casually into the songs. I like the deft rhyming of the song that is always sung in the last act by two comedians and a comedienne.'
DOROTHY PARKER

As the curtain opens on this act, the American musicals were either musical burlesques of current unmusical theatrical productions (Weber and Fields) or heavy imported, usually Viennese, operettas which were neither humorous nor colourful. As a result, the American musical very much resembled a bunch of gaily-costumed vaudeville specialists hired to do their renowned routines.

Enter Elisabeth Marbury, a charming, resourceful literary agent who convinces manager-producer F. Ray Comstock to produce a miniature musical. Have two sets or less, she suggested, eleven musicians, a small cast, and a strong book. Too, see that the music and lyrics further the plot, or even, explain the characters.

The plot thickens: drama critics are astounded, then delighted. The shows contain humorous situations, funny dialogue, enchanting melodies, and clever lyrics. They became known as the Princess shows, and established the reputations of book writer Guy Bolton, book and lyric writer P.G. Wodehouse, and composer Jerome Kern.

PGW made his American theatrical bow under the auspices of distinguished colleagues. The colossal theatre owners/booking agents in American theatre history were Marc Klaw and Abraham Lincoln Erlanger, who controlled over 700 theatres. Their leading producers were Henry W. Savage, Charles Dillingham, and Florenz Ziegfeld. PGW continued this impressive opening by working with every major theatre-composer of his time.

It was a strange combination, this theatrical triumvirate, with unusual collaborative methods. Songs, for example, had out-of-the ordinary origins. Jerome Kern would supply a melody to PGW who, not being able to read music, would fashion 'dummy' lyrics to the rhythm on the spot (dum-dum-da-dum). Later on, he would then create his genuine lyric, which would of course fit the melody perfectly. Equally unorthodox was PGW's work as a librettist. Guy Bolton provided the bones of the plot, and PGW furnished the meat of dialogue and characterization.

Wodehouse and Bolton usually shared a 5% royalty for their book and lyric collaborations, while PGW received a variable flat fee for his lyrical interpolations.

Nowhere is PGW's skill more evident than in his adaptations of foreign plays, an effort especially laudable in light of his ignorance of any language other than English. His agent would provide PGW with a translation, usually only a plot synopsis. And PGW would embellish accordingly.

His theatre and his novels were firmly linked in PGW's world. Bolton took a Wodehouse novel, *Spring Fever*, and transformed it into the outline for a play,

Out of Nowhere, which changed the leading man to a woman and the locale from England to Hollywood. PGW later changed the play back to a successful novel, *The Old Reliable*, which retained the female lead and the setting. Indeed, most of Wodehouse's early novels were similar to plays, rich in dialogue and characterization. Also the theatre formed the background for several of his works; and several of his works were backgrounds for plays (*A Gentleman of Leisure*, *A Damsel in Distress*, *Leave it to Psmith*, *Who's Who* and *The Inside Stand*). All evidence of a career so firmly linked to the theatre as to be inseparable.

Miss Springtime

Although Ziegfeld used its roof garden for his midnight extravaganzas, the New Amsterdam Theatre was the headquarters of the Klaw and Erlanger empire. The musicals were as lavish as the producers were powerful.

Miss Springtime's opening night playbill, which lists the Klaw and Erlanger partnership as a 'construction company'.

Fame is imminent; the trio in 1916. Guy Bolton is standing over the seated PGW while Jerome Kern lights a cigarette.

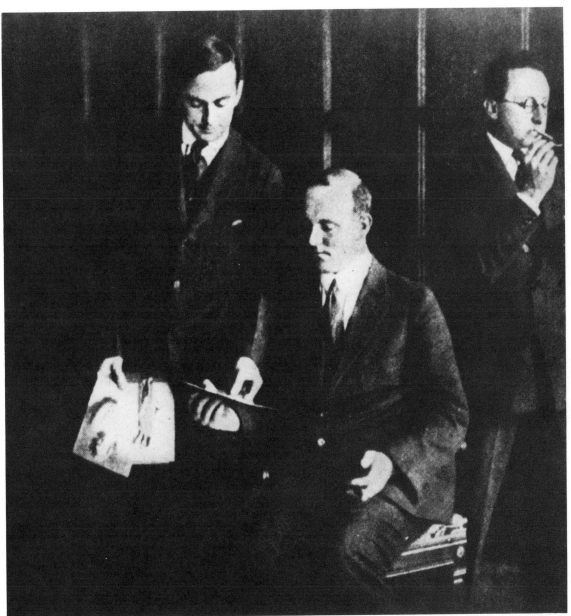

Julian Mitchell, right, who was the choreographer of four Bolton-Wodehouse-Kern shows, including *Miss Springtime*, had a slight occupational impediment – he was extremely hard of hearing.

Theatrical scenic and lighting designer Joseph Urban, recipient of numerous awards; he was an Austrian who revolutionized the American musical stage.

One of PGW's hits from the show.

Throw · Me · A · Rose

1915

Miss Springtime

Book · by · Guy · Bolton
Music · by · Emmerich · Kalman
Lyrics · by · P. G. Wodehouse
and Herbert Reynolds

Klaw & Erlanger's Successful Production

VOCAL

A Little Country Mouse	.60
A Little Bid For Sympathy	.60
The Love Monopoly	.60
In The Garden Of Romance	.60
These Are The Words	.60
Throw Me A Rose	.60
Life Is A Game Of Bluff	.60

INSTRUMENTAL

Selection	1.00

T. B. HARMS

AND
FRANCIS, DAY & HUNTER
NEW YORK

Burton Rice

A Kern interpolation, sung by an original cast member. MacFarlane was hired for the show because he·was an established record artist.

Miss Springtime

25 September 1916 (227 performances)
New Amsterdam Theatre, New York

Producer: Klaw and Erlanger
Book: Guy Bolton
Music: Emmerich Kalman and Jerome Kern
Lyrics: P.G. Wodehouse and Herbert Reynolds
Director: Herbert Gresham
Choreographer: Julian Mitchell
Scenery: Joseph Urban
Musical Director: Charles Previn

Cast

Paul Pilgrim, editor	CHARLES MEAKINS
Michael Robin, his assistant	JOHN E. HAZZARD
Katski Schmidt, Rosi's maiden aunt	JOSIE INTROPODI
Henry Wenzel, druggist and postmaster	NICK BURNHAM
Hugo Knaus, 'native son'	MAURICÉ CASS
Rosika Wenzel, Henry's daughter	SARI PETRASS (*from the Kiraly Theatre, Budapest*)
Jo Varady, a gypsy photographer	GEORGE MacFARLANE
Maimie Stone, from New York	GEORGIA O'RAMEY
Dustin Stone, a rich American	JED PROUTY
Officer	WILLIAM COHAN
Inspector Block, of Budapest	PERCY WOODLEY
Secretary to Rudolph Marto	WAYNE NUNN
Maitre de Ballet	FRED NICE
Première Danseuse	ADA WEEKS
Russie	AUDREY BURTON
Cessie	BILLIE VERNON

Act I   Old Home Week in the village of Pilota
Act II   Wenzel's Apothecary Shop, Pilota
Act III The stage of the Budapest Opera House

Musical Numbers:
ACT I
1 'Throw Me a Rose' *Pilgrim & Robin*
2 'Sunrise'
3 'This is the Existence' *Robin & Committee of Six*
4 'Once Upon a Time' *Rosika Wenzel*
5 'Life is a Game of Bluff' *Robin & Varady*
6 'A Bid for Sympathy' *Pilgrim & Rosika*
7 Finale
ACT II
1 Opening – Ensemble
2 'The Love Monopoly' *Varady & girls*
3 'My Castle in the Air' *Rosika & men*
4 'A Very Good Girl on Sunday' *Maimle Stone & girls*
5 'Some One' *Rosika*
6 Burletta – 'The Oold-Fashioned Drama' *Maimie, Dustin & Robin*
7 'The Garden of Romance' *Varady & Rosika*
8 Finale
ACT III
1 Opening Ballet
  (a) 'The Dance of Isis' *Ensemble*
  (b) 'Dance Eccentrique' *Maitre de Ballet & Première Danseuse*
2 'A Country Mouse' *Rosika & Ensemble*
3 'When You're Full of Talk' *Robin*
4 'Some One' *Varady, Pilgrim & Rosika*
5 Finale

Published lyrics by PGW:
Vocal Score
My Castle in the Air
Once Upon a Time (in vocal score)
Saturday Night
This is the Existence (in vocal score)
Throw Me a Rose
A Very Good Girl on Sunday (same as *Saturday Night*)
When You're Full of Talk

Have a Heart

Have a Heart

11 January 1917 (78 performances)
Liberty Theatre, New York

Producer: Henry W. Savage
Book: Guy Bolton and P.G. Wodehouse
Music: Jerome Kern
Lyrics: P.G. Wodehouse
Director: Edward Royce
Scenery: Henry Ives Cobb, Jr.
Musical Director: Gustave Salzer

Cast

Henry, the elevator boy	BILLY B. VAN
Ted Sheldon	DONALD MacDONALD
Lizzie O'Brien	MARJORIE GATESON
Det. Baker, of the Blueport police	EUGENE KEITH
Rutherford Schoonmaker, prop.	THURSTON HALL
Capt. Charles Owen	ROY GORDON
Peggy Schoonmaker	EILEEN VAN BIENE
Mrs. Pyne, Peggy's Aunt	FLAVIA ARCARO
Matthew Pyne	JAMES BRADBURY
Dolly Brabazon	LOUISE DRESSER
Yussuf, the entertainer	JOSEPH DEL PUENTE
Maitre d'Hotel	EUGENE REVERE
Georgia	PEGGY FEARS

Act I   Lingerie room at Schoonmaker's
Act II   Scene 1 – Lounge of the Ocean View Hotel
         Night.
         Scene 2 – The Same. Next Morning
Place – Blueport, R.I.   Time – The Present

Musical Numbers:

ACT I
1 'Shop' *Salesgirls*
2 'I'm So Busy' *Lizzie & Ted*
3 'Have a Heart' *Ruddy*
4 'I Am All Alone' *Ruddy & Peggy*
5 'I'm Here, Little Girl, I'm Here' *Ted & Girls*
6 'Bright Lights' *Dolly & Henry*
7 'The Road That Lies Before' *Ruddy & Peggy*
8 Finale
ACT II
1 (a) Opening Chorus *Guests*
  (b) 'Samarkand' *Yussuf & Ensemble*
2 'Honeymoon Inn' *Peggy & Ensemble*
3 'Come Out of the Kitchen' *Dolly*
4 'My Wife-My Man' *Peggy & Ruddy*
5 'You Said Something' *Ted, Lizzie & Ensemble*
6 Dance Duet *Ted & Georgia*
7 'Napoleon' *Henry, Flunkeys & Girls*
8 'Peter Pan' *Peggy*
9 Finale *Ensemble*

Published lyrics by PGW:
Vocal Score
And I Am All Alone
Bright Lights (in vocal score only)
Daisy
Have a Heart
Honeymoon Inn
I'm Here, Little Girls, I'm Here (in vocal score only)
I'm So Busy
Napoleon
Polly Believed in Preparedness
The Road That Lies Before
Samarkand (in vocal score only)
They All Look Alike
You Said Something

HENRY W. SAVAGE
offers
The Musical Comedy
HAVE
A
HEART
BOOK AND LYRICS BY
GUY BOLTON &
P.G. WODEHOUSE
MUSIC BY
JEROME KERN

The publicity brochure for the touring company,
which, in this instance, was the original Broadway
cast. *Have A Heart* lasted only three months in New
York. It toured the country for over five years.

Dolly
and
Henry

Dolly
and
Matthew

Dancing
Duo

Louise Dresser, Eugene Revere, and Billy B. Van at
table; Louise Dresser and James Bradbury seated;
Peggy Fears and Donald MacDonald, featured
dancers.

"Ah, Say! Have A Heart"

"Napoleon"

(And I, Take After

Nap)

Vaudeville star Billy B. Van is surrounded by chorus
girls during his rendition of 'Napoleon', the first of
PGW's history-kidding lyrics.

The birthplace of American musical comedy. The 299-seat, Shubert-owned Princess is located on the South side of 39th Street, between Broadway and 6th Avenue.

Left to right: Co-producer Morris Gest, PGW, Guy Bolton, co-producer and Princess Theatre co-founder Ray Comstock, and Jerome Kern.

"Oh, Boy," the fourth of
heir origin in the famous
Princess Theatre produc-
d the audience in the
zation of the ideal in
ffering, interspersed
with the prettiest
odern gowns.
the smart
This

The most successful
B-W-K collaboration,
Oh, Boy! was also the
team's first Princess
production.

Oh, Boy!

20 February 1917 (475 performances)
Princess Theatre, New York

Producer: Comstock-Elliott Company
Book: Guy Bolton and P.G. Wodehouse
Music: Jerome Kern
Lyrics: P.G.Wodehouse
Director: Edward Royce
Musical Director: Max Hirschfield

Cast

Briggs, George's valet	CARL LYLE
Jane Packard	MARION DAVIES
Polly Andrus	JUSTINE JOHNSTONE
Jim Marvin	HAL FORDE
George Budd	TOM POWERS
Lou Ellen Carter	MARIE CARROLL
Jackie Sampson	ANNA WHEATON
Constable Simms	STEPHEN MALEY
Judge Daniel Carter	FRANK McGINN
Mrs. Carter	AUGUSTA HAVILAND
Miss Penelope Budd	EDNA MAY OLIVER
A Club Waiter	JACK MERRITT
Miss Lottie Limmut	JEANETTE COOKE
Miss Iona Saxon	PATRICE CLARKE
Miss Rhoda Byke	EVELYN GRIEG
Miss Sheila Ryve	MARGARET MASON
Miss Inna Ford	ANNA STONE
Miss Georgia Spelvin	FLORENCE McGUIRE
Miss Wanda Farr	KATHERINE HURST
Miss Anna Thrope	ETHEL FORDE
Miss Billie Dew	LILLIAN RICE
Miss Lotta Noyes	KATHRYN RAHN
Miss Annie Olde-Knight	LILLIAN LAVONNE
Miss B. Ava Little	MARJORIE ROLLAND
Miss Delia Kards	VERA MEYERS
Mr. Olaf Lauder	AUSTIN CLARK
Mr. Ivan L. Ovanerve	ALDEN GLOVER, Jr.
Mr. Will Hooper Rupp	JOSEPH HADLEY
Mr. Phil Ossify	CHARLES YORKSHIRE
Mr. Phelan Fyne	RALPH O'BRIEN
Mr. Hugo Chaseit	CLARENCE LUTZ

Act I   Scene 1 – the Bachelor apartment of George Budd, at Meadowsides, Long Island. Night
Scene 2 – The Same. Next morning
Act II   The Meadowsides Country Club. Afternoon of the same day

Musical Numbers:

ACT I. Scene 1
1 (a) Scene: Music.
   (b) Ensemble – 'Let's Make a Night of It' *Jim & Ensemble*
2 'You Never Knew About Me' *Lou Ellen & George*
3 'A Package of Seeds' *Jim, Jane, Polly & Girls*
4 'An Old-Fashioned Wife' *Lou Ellen & Girls*
5 'A Pal Like You' *Jackie & Jim*
6 'Till the Clouds Roll By' *Jackie & George*
ACT I. Scene 2
7 'A Little Bit of Ribbon' *Jane & Girls*
8 'The First Day of May' *Jackie, Jim & George*
9 Finale *The Company*
ACT II
10 'Koo-La-Loo' *Jim & Ensemble*
11 Dance *Miss Dickson & Mr. Hyson*
12 'Rolled Into One' *Jackie & Ensemble*
13 'Oh, Daddy, Please!' *Lou Ellen, George & Judge Carter*
14 'Nesting Time' *Jackie & Jim*
15 'Words Are Not Needed' *Lou Ellen & Boys*
16 'Flubby Dub, the Cave-Man' *Jackie, Jim & George*
17 Finale *The Company*

Published lyrics by PGW:

Ain't It a Grand and Glorious Feeling
Be a Little Sunbeam
Every Day (same as *Words Are Not Needed*)
Nesting Time in Flatbush
An Old Fashioned Wife
A Package of Seeds
A Pal Like You
Rolled Into One
Till the Clouds Roll By
We're Going to be Pals
Words Are Not Needed
You Never Knew About Me

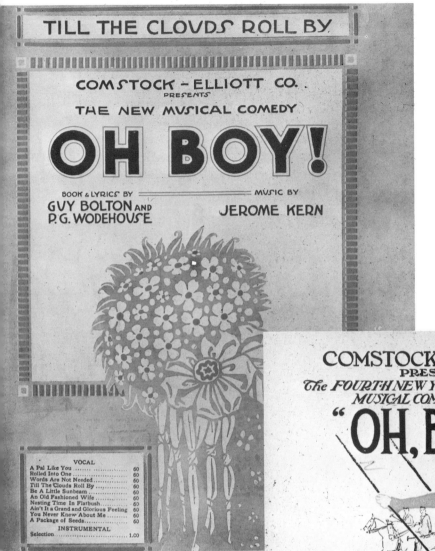

The show's most
popular song, later the
title of Kern's movie
autobiography.

Publicity card.

Oh, Joy!

27 January 1919 (167 performances)
Kingsway Theatre, London

Producers: George Grossmith and Edward Laurillard
Director: Austen Hurgon
Musical Director: Leonard Hornsey

Cast

Briggs	HAL GORDON
Jane Packard	ISABEL JEANS
Polly Andrus	JUDITH NELMES
Jim Marvin	BILLY LEONARD
George Budd	TOM POWERS (his original part in America)
Lou Ellen Carter	DOT TEMPLE
Jackie Sampson	BEATRICE LILLIE
Constable Simms	FRED RUSSELL
Sir John Carter, J.P.	TOM PAYNE
Lady Carter	DIANA DURAND
Miss Penelope Budd	HELEN ROUS
A Club Waiter	LUCIEN MUSSIERE

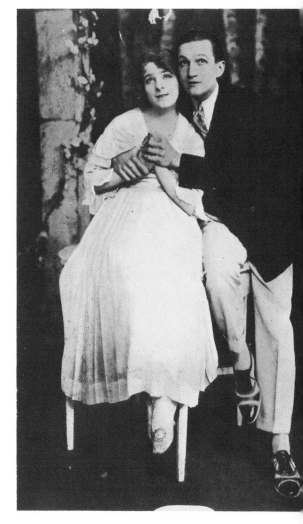

Dot Temple and Tom Powers, romantic leads of the retitled English production. American star Powers followed his role to England.

Right: Bea Lillie and Billy Leonard, comic stars of *Oh, Joy!*; this marked Miss Lillie's debut in what was to be a most distinguished career in the theatre.

Leave it to Jane

Leave it to Jane

28 August 1917 (167 performances)
Longacre Theatre, New York

Producers: William Elliott, F. Ray Comstock and
    Morris Gest
Book: Guy Bolton and P.G. Wodehouse (founded on
    'The College Widow' by George Ade)
Music: Jerome Kern
Lyrics: P.G. Wodehouse
Director: Edward Royce
Choreographer: David Bennett
Musical Director: John McGhie

Cast

Ollie Mitchell, a sophomore	RULOFF CUTTEN
Matty McGowan, a trainer	DAN COLLYER
'Stub' Talmadge, a busy undergraduate	OSCAR SHAW
'Silent' Murphy, a center rush	THOMAS DELMAR
Bessie Tanner, an athletic girl	ANN ORR
Sally Cameron, a co-ed	JANE CARROLL
Peter Witherspoon, president	FREDERICK GRAHAM
Howard Talbot, a tutor	ALGERNON GRIEG
Jane Witherspoon, daughter of the president	EDITH HALLOR
Jimsey Hopper, a student	HARRY FORBES
Dick McAllister, another student	D.E. CHARLES
Flora Wiggins, a prominent waitress	GEORGIA O'RAMEY
Hiram Bolton	WILL C. CRIMANS
Billy Bolton, a half-back	ROBERT G. PITKIN
Hon. Elam Hicks, of Scwantumville	ALAN KELLY
Harold ('Bub') Hicks, a freshman	OLIN HOWLAND

Act I   Atwater College. The terrace of Memorial
            Hall on the opening day of the fall term
Act II   Outside the football field

Musical Numbers:

ACT I Scene 1.
1 Atwater College Songs *Male Ensemble*
2 'A Peach of a Life' *Stub & Bessie*
3 'Wait Till To-morrow' *Jane & Boys*
4 'Watch My Step' *Stub, Louella & Girls*
5 'Leave It To Jane' *Jane, Stub, Bessie & Girls*
6 'The Crickets Are Calling' *Jane & Billy*
ACT I Scene 2.
7 Medley of College Songs *Principals & Ensemble*
8 'When the Orchestra's Playing Your Favorite Waltz' *Billy & Town Girls*
9 'Cleopatterer' *Flora*
10 'Something to Say' *Jane & Billy*
11 Finale
ACT II
12 Football Song *Bessie & Ensemble*
13 (a) 'The Days of Chivalry' *Stub, Flora & Bub*
    (b) Reprise of Football Song *Ensemble*
14 'I'm So Happy' *Bessie & Stub*
15 'The Siren Song' *Jane, Bessie & Girls*
16 'I'm Going To Find a Girl Some Day' *Stub, Bub, Ollie & Girls*
17 Finale

Published lyrics by PGW:

Vocal Score
Cleopatterer
The Crickets Are Calling
I'm Going To Find a Girl
It's a Great Big Land
Just You Watch My Step
Leave It To Jane
A Peach of a Life
Poor Prune
Sir Galahad
The Siren's Song
The Sun Shines Brighter
There It Is Again
Wait Till Tomorrow (in vocal score only)
What I'm Longing To Say
Why?

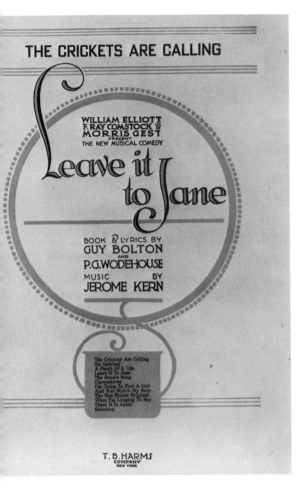

The College Widow, a play by American newspaper humorist George Ade and a staple in the straight comedy repertoire, provided the foundation for *Leave it to Jane*.

Oscar Shaw, handsome leading man in three PGW shows, started his climb to fame as a 'busy undergraduate'.

PLAYGRAM

JANUARY
1960

SHERIDAN SQUARE
PLAYHOUSE
7th AVE. & 4th STREET, NEW YORK

LEAVE IT
TO JANE

Leave it to Jane

25 May 1959 (928 performances)
Sheridan Square Playhouse, New York

Producers: Joseph Beruh and Peter Katz
Director: Lawrence Carra
Choreographer: Mary Jane Doerr
Musical Director: Joseph Stecko

Cast

Ollie Mitchell	AUSTIN O'TOOLE
Matty McGowan	MONROE ARNOLD
'Stub' Talmadge	ANGELO MANGO
'Silent' Murphy	BERNIE MEYER
Peter Witherspoon	JON RICHARDS
Bessie Tanner	JEANNE ALLEN
Flora Wiggins	DOROTHY GREENER
Howard Talbot	BERT POLLOCK
Jane Witherspoon	KATHLEEN MURRAY
Hiram Bolton	MARC JORDAN
Billy Bolton	DAVID STARKEY
Hon. Elan Hicks	ALEK PRIMROSE
Harold 'Bub' Hicks	LANE SMITH

I DON'T WORK IN THE TENDERLOIN

I'M DOROTHY GREENER AND I'M IN LEAVE IT TO JANE AT THE SHERIDAN SQ. PLAYHOUSE 7th Ave. & W. 4th St., CH 2-9609

Kathleen Murray, seated, listens to Dorothy Greener admonish Angelo Mango in this playgram from the 1959 Off-Broadway revival.

Her performance of the show-stopping 'Cleopatterer' was unsurpassed; Dorothy Greener's 'Flora' was one reason for this revival's tremendous success. And this clever newspaper advertisement also pulled in the crowds, to chalk up a record run of 928 performances.

53

AN ORIGINAL CAST RECORDING

JOSEPH BERUH
and
PETER KATZ
present

Leave it to Jane

Book and Lyrics by
GUY BOLTON
and
P. G. WODEHOUSE

Music by
JEROME KERN

Featuring:

KATHLEEN   DOROTHY
MURRAY   GREENER

ANGELO   JEANNE   ART
MANGO   ALLEN   MATTHEWS

MUSICAL DIRECTOR:
JOSEPH STECKO

Production Directed by
LAWRENCE CARRA

Album Music Arrangements—ART HARRIS
Produced for records by MARV HOLTZMAN
Choreographer—MARY JANE DOERR
Settings by LLOYD BURLINGAME
Costumes by AL LEHMAN
Lighting by GEORGE CORRIN
Assistant Director: GIGI CASCIO

Presented at
SHERIDAN SQ. PLAYHOUSE

Kitty Darlin'

10 September 1917
Teck Theatre, Buffalo, New York

Producers: William Elliott, F. Ray Comstock and
    Morris Gest
Book: Guy Bolton and P.G.Wodehouse (founded on
    'Sweet Kitty Bellairs' by David Belasco)
Music: Rudolf Friml
Lyrics: P.G. Wodehouse
Director: Edward Royce
Musical Director: William Axt

Cast

Prologue spoken by	Miss RAY WELLESLEY
Sir Jasper Standish	JACKSON HINES
Col. the Hon. Henry Villiers	EDWIN STEVENS
Capt. Spicer	FRANK WESTERTON
Lieut. Lord Verney	JOHN PHILLIPS
Lieut. Tom Stafford	JOHN HOPE
Gandy	H. JESS SMITH
Col. Kimby McFinton	GEORGE CALLAHAN
Capt. Dennis O'Hara	TEN EYCK CLAY
Major Owney McTeague	C. TIEMAN
Lieut. Lanty McClusky	WILLIAM REID
Mallow	FRANK BRADLEY
Lady Julia Standish	JUANITA FLETCHER
Lady Maria Prideaux	PAULINE HALL
Lady Bab Flyte	SIDONIA ESPERO
Lydie	ELEANOR DANIELS
Mistress Kitty Bellairs	ALICE NIELSEN

Act I   The gardens at Prideaux Hall
Act II   Lord Verney's lodgings. Four o'clock in the
           morning
Act III The Great Gallery at Prideaux Hall

Musical Numbers:
ACT I
1 Opening Chorus
2 O'Hara & Debutantes
3 Trio *Lady Bab, Jasper & Spicer*
4 The Mother of the Regiment *Kitty & Irish Officers*
5 'Dear Curracloe' *Kitty*
6 Duet *Kitty & Julia*
7 Finale
ACT II
1 Duet *Mallow & Lydia*
2 'Noah' *Villiers & Male Chorus*

3 'Peggy's Leg' *Villiers & Officers*
4 Duet *Kitty & Verney*
ACT III
1 Opening Chorus
2 Solo Dance – 'Vanity' *Miss Doris Faithful*
3 Song *O'Hara & Debutantes*
4 'Tick, Tick, Tick' *Kitty & Ensemble*
5 'The Dawn of Love' *Kitty & Verney*
6 'Dublin' *Kitty & Officers*
Dramatic Scene *Kitty, Verney & Ensemble*
Finale

Unfortunately, this opened and closed in Buffalo, New York. It featured opera star Alice Nielsen.

The same production company as for *Miss Springtime* was gathered for this show.

The Riviera Girl

24 September 1917 (78 performances)
New Amsterdam Theatre, New York

Producers: Klaw and Erlanger
Book: Guy Bolton and P.G. Wodehouse
Music: Emmerich Kalman and Jerome Kern
Lyrics: P.G. Wodehouse
Director: Herbert Gresham
Choreographer: Julian Mitchell
Scenery: Joseph Urban
Musical Director: Charles Previn

Cast

Sylva Bareska, a vaudeville singer	WILDA BENNETT
Baron Ferrier, an ex-Ambassador	J. CLARENCE HARVEY
Charles Lorenz	ARTHUR BURCKLEY
Gustave, proprietor of the Côte d'Azur	EUGENE LOCKHART
Anatole (English), a waiter	FRANK FARRINGTON
Sam Springer	SAM HARDY
Birdie Springer, his wife	JULIETTE DAY
Count Michael Lorenz	LOUIS CASAVANT
Cleo	BESSIE GROSS
Julie	FLORENCE DELMAR
Lucile	MAE CARMEN
Babette	ETHEL DELMAR
Victor de Berryl	CARL GANTVOORT
Old Rigg	WILLIAM SADLER
Claire Ferrier	VIOLA CAIN
The Butterfly	MARJORIE BENTLEY
Daisy	MARJORIE BENTLEY
Paul	J. LOWE MURPHY
The New Star	LOUISE EVANS

Act I   Garden Theatre of the Côte d'Azur, Theatre of Varieties, Monte Carlo. Night
Act II   Flower fete in the Garden of Ferrier's Villa, Monte Carlo. Afternoon
Act III A Revue. 'Nights' Revelries' in the rotunda of the Côte d'Azur, Theatre of Varieties, Monte Carlo. Night

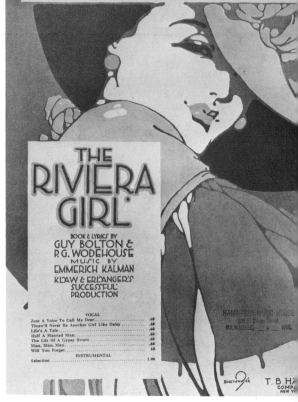

Musical Numbers:
ACT I
1 Opening song and chorus *Sylva & Chorus*
2 'Sometimes I Feel Just Like Grandpa' *Sam & Girls*
3 'The Fall of Man' *Sylva & Charles*
4 'There'll Never Be Another Girl Like Daisy' *Count, Ferrier & Male Chorus*
5 'Life's a Tale' *Sylva & Victor*
6 Finale *Principals & Chorus*
ACT II
7 Opening Chorus *Butterfly & Chorus*
8 'Just a Voice to Call Me Dear' *Sylva & Men*
9 'Half a Married Man' *Victor & Girls*
10 'Man, Man, Man' *Victor, Sylva, Claire & Charles*
11 'Let's Build a Little Bungalow in Quogue' *Sam & Birdie*
12 'Will You Forget' *Sylva & Victor*
13 Finale *Principals & Chorus*
ACT III
14 Opening Revue
15 'Why Don't They Hand it to Me?' *Sam & Girls*
16 'Gypsy, Bring Your Fiddle' *Sylva & Chorus*
17 Finale *Principals & Chorus*

Published lyrics by PGW:
Half a Married Man
Just a Voice to Call Me, Dear
Let's Build a Little Bungalow in Quogue
Life's a Tale
The Lilt of a Gypsy Strain
Man, Man, Man
There'll Never Be Another Girl Like Daisy
Will You Forget?

Miss 1917

5 November 1917 (48 performances)
Century Theatre, New York

Producers: Charles Dillingham and Florenz Ziegfeld, Jr.
Book: Guy Bolton and P.G. Wodehouse
Music: Victor Herbert and Jerome Kern
Lyrics: P.G. Wodehouse
Director: Ned Wayburn
Scenery: Joseph Urban
Musical Director: Robert Hood Bowers

ACT I
The Society Farmerettes (Herbert) *Vivienne Segal & Farmerettes*
'Crooks' (Kern) *Cecil Lean & Harry Kelly*
'Papa Would Persist in Picking Peaches' (Kern) *Andrew Tombes, Zitelka Dolores, Yvonne Shelton & Peaches*
'Tell Me All Your Troubles, Cutie' (Kern) *Elizabeth Brice & Charles King*
'A Dancing M.D.' (Kern) *George White, Vera Maxwell, Marion Davies, Emma Haig*
Travesty *Harry Kelly & Vivienne Segal*
'A Dancing Courtship' *George White & Ann Pennington*
Maja Dance *Tortola Valencia*
'Who's Zoo in Girl Land' (Kern) *Andrew Tombes & 'animals'*
Songs *Gus Van & Joe Schenck*
'The Old Man in the Moon' (Kern) *Bessie McCoy Davis*
A Chance Meeting *Savoy & Brennan*
'The Land Where the Good Songs Go' (Kern) *Elizabeth Brice & Charles King*
Finale
ACT II
Falling leaves *Adolf Bolm*
'We Want to Laugh' (Kern) *Bessie McCoy Davis & Girls*
The Singing Blacksmith of Curriclough *Stephen O'Rourke*
'The Beauty Doctor' (Herbert) *Cecil Lean & Cleo Mayfield*
Dancing Specialty *Ann Pennington*
'The Palm Beach Girl' (Kern) *Cecil Lean & Cleo Mayfield*
Dreamland *Irene Castle*
'That's the Picture I Want to See' (Kern) *Elizabeth Brice & Charles King*

Dance Imitation *George White*
'You're the Little Girl I've Looked So Long For' (Kern) *Andrew Tombes & Vivienne Segal*
Finale

Published lyrics by PGW:
Go, Little Boat
I'm the Old Man in the Moon
The Land Where the Good Songs Go
Peaches
The Picture I want to See
Tell Me All Your Troubles, Cutie
We're Crooks

No less than Charles Dillingham and Florenz Ziegfeld created this monumental fiasco. A lavish production, *Miss 1917* would have lost between three and four thousand dollars a week if it had sold out every night. Nevertheless, it was one of five shows that Wodehouse had running on Broadway at the same time.

Van & Schenck Ned Wayburn Harry Kelly Andrew Tombes

George White Lew Fields Cecil Lean Charles King

Arthur Cunningham Gene Revere

Savoy & Brennan Adolf Bolm Joseph M. Sparks Robert Hood Bowers

This overwhelming array of masculine talent was
partially responsible for the over-extended budget.
Lew Fields, formerly of Weber and Fields, headlined
this galaxy of stars.

Irene Castle, of the popular ballroom dance team Irene and Vernon Castle, received top salary for her nightly twenty-second-long appearance.

Assorted speciality singers, actresses, and showgirls from this mammoth flop.

Cleo Mayfield

Flora Revalles

Elizabeth Brice

Vivienne Segal

Marion Davies

Ann Pennington

Oh, Lady! Lady!!

1 February 1918 (219 performances)
Princess Theatre, New York

Producers: F. Ray Comstock and William Elliott
Book: Guy Bolton and P.G. Wodehouse
Music: Jerome Kern
Lyrics: P.G. Wodehouse
Directors: Robert Milton and Edward Royce
Musical Director: Max Hirschfeld

Cast

Parker	CONSTANCE BINNEY
Mollie Farringdon	VIVIENNE SEGAL
Mrs. Farringdon	MARGARET DALE
Willoughby Finch	CARL RANDALL
Hale Underwood	HARRY C. BROWNE
Spike Hudgins, Finch's valet	EDWARD ABELES
Fanny Welch	FLORENCE SHIRLEY
May Barber	CARROLL McCOMAS
Cyril Twombley	REGINALD MASON
William Watty	HARRY FISHER
Miss Lettice Romayne	LOIS WHITNEY
Miss Lotta Pommery	BOBBY BREWSTER
Miss Della Catessen	MAY ELSIE
Miss Hallie Butt	ELSIE LEWIS
Miss Sal Munn	DOROTHY ALLAN
Miss Marie Schino	BILLIE BOOKER
Miss Mollie Gatawney	MILDRED FISHER
Miss Marion Etta Herring	EDNA HETTLER
Miss C. Ella Rhy	GYPSEY MOONEY
Miss Barbara O'Rhum	MILDRED ROLAND
Miss Clarette Cupp	JEANNE SPARRY
Miss May Anne Ayes	MABEL STANFORD
Miss Cassie Roll	JANET VELIE
Miss Virginia Hamm	BETTIE GEREAUX
Mr. Artie C. Hoke	WILLIAM WALSH
Mr. B. Russell Sprout	CHARLES HARTMAN
Mr. C. Ollie Flower	CHARLES COLUMBUS
Mr. H. Ash-Brown	J. RANDALL PHELAN
Mr. Stewart Prune	JACK VINCENT
Mr. Con Kearney	IRVING JACKSON

Act I   Living Room of the Farringdon Place at Hempstead, L.I.
Act II   Roof Garden of Willoughby Finch's Studio in Waverly Mews

Musical Numbers:

ACT I
1 (a) Scene Music
   (b) 'I'm To Be Married To-day' *Molly & Girls*
2 'Not Yet' *Molly & Willoughby*
3 'Do It Now' *Hale, Spike & Willoughby*
4 'Our Little Nest' *Spike & Fanny*
5 'Do Look At Him' *Molly & Girls*
6 'Oh, Lady! Lady!! *Will & Girls*
7 'You Found Me and I Found You' *May & Underwood*
8 Finaletto *Company Ensemble*
ACT II
9 Opening – 'Moon' *Miss Sparry & Ensemble*
   Dance *Miss Binney & Mr. Phelan*
10 'Waiting Around the Corner' *May & Boys*
11 'Little Ships Come Sailing Home' *Molly & Girls*
12 'Before I Met You' *Will & Molly*
13 'Greenwich Village' *Will, Spike & Fanny*
14 'Wheatless Days' *Underwood & May*
15 'It's a Hard, Hard World for a Man' *Will, Underwood & Twombley*
16 Finale *Ensemble*

Published lyrics by PGW:

Vocal Score
Before I Met You
Bill
Dear Old Prison Days
Do It Now (in vocal score only)
Do Look At Him (in vocal score only)
Greenwich Village
It's a Hard, Hard World For a Man
Moon Song
Not Yet
Oh, Lady! Lady!!
Our Little Nest
A Picture I Want to See
Some Little Girl
The Sun Starts to Shine Again
Waiting Round the Corner
Wheatless Days
When the Ships Come Home
You Found Me and I Found You

Beginning the New year with a bang, and following on the heels of *Oh Boy!*, *Oh Lady! Lady!!* was the Princess' newest crown.

"OH LADY.! LADY!"
IS THE 5TH N.Y. PRINCESS THEATRE MUSICAL COMEDY SUCCESS
by
BOLTON, WODEHOUSE AND KERN
WHO ALSO WROTE
NOBODY HOME - VERY GOOD EDDIE - OH BOY
AND LEAVE IT TO JANE

"'OH, LADY! LADY!!' makes big hit at Princess. Daintiest of Musical Plays proves to be a fitting successor to 'OH, BOY!' The Princess Theatre undertook a task that must have presented the greatest difficulties. They went out to find a new musical play that would become a fitting successor to their own 'OH, BOY!' which was the best piece of its kind that New York had seen in a dozen years. To come directly to the point, they were entirely successful. 'OH, LADY! LADY!!' in short, is the epitome of good taste."—*Louis De Foe, N.Y. World.*

"'OH, LADY! LADY!!' adds another success to the Princess list. Musical Entertainment of the Worthiest Type. You may score another hit for the Princess Theatre without fear of having to run a black mark through the record after you have seen 'OH, LADY! LADY!!' Not the slightest question of its immediate success. And tuneful it is to a degree. Practically every one of the songs was an encore number and no one of them is without distinction in the matter of lyrics."
—*Burns Mantle, N. Y. Evening Mail.*

"'OH, LADY! LADY!!' is after 'OH, BOY!' Another Musical Comedy of the Princess Theatre Type Scores Heavily. A good story, clever lines, tasteful music, and girls long on grace and refinement. Once more Comstock & Elliott have shown their allegiance to the policy of supplying popular entertainment, which is mitigated by all available talent and good taste."—*New York Times.*

Staged by
ROBERT MILTON and EDWARD ROYCE

Below: leading men Carl Randall, Edward Abeles, and Harry C. Browne behind chorus cuties.

See You Later

15 April 1918
Academy of Music, Baltimore, Maryland

Producer: A.H. Woods
Book: Guy Bolton and P.G. Wodehouse (based on
    Pierre Veber's farce, *The Girl from Rector's*)
Music: Jean Schwartz and William F. Peters
Lyrics: P.G. Wodehouse
Director: Robert Milton
Musical Director: Eugene Salzer

Cast

Sam, waiter at The Chateau	JAMES E. SULLIVAN
Commodore 'Johnny' Walker	HERBERT CORTHELL
Jane Packard	TOT QUALTERS
Polly Andrews	BETTY ALDEN
Dickson Paige	CHARLES RUGGLES (courtesy of Oliver Morosco)
Jo Romaine	MABEL McCANE
Sheriff Sims	WILLIAM SELLERY
Lord Glenochtie	ERNEST TORRENCE
Mrs. Wellington Green	CHARLOTTE GRANVILLE
Bettina Weston, her daughter	MARIE FLYNN
Horace Blossom, her cousin	JOHN DALY MURPHY
George Potter, another cousin	JED PROUTY
Mrs. Honora Blossom	ISABEL O'MADIGAN
Angelique, maid	ZITELKA DOLORES

Act I   'The Chateau' near Great Neck, Long Island
Act II   Mrs. Wellington Green's house, Utica, New
       York
Act III 'The Chateau'

Musical Numbers:

ACT I
1 Opening number *Ensemble*
2 'I'm Going to Settle Down' *Dicky & Ensemble*
3 'If You Could Read My Mind' *Jo, Commodore & Dicky*
4 'Keep Out of the Moon' *Betty & Ensemble*
5 'No One Ever Loved Like Me' *Betty & Dicky*
6 'The Finest Thing in the Country' *Jo & Ensemble*
7 Finale *Company & Ensemble*

ACT II
8 Opening Cantata *Potter, Mrs. Green, Mr. Blossom, Mrs. Blossom & Ensemble*
9 'Young Man' *Dicky, Mrs. Green, Mr. Potter, Mrs. Blossom, Mr. Blossom*
10 'Honeymoon Island' *Betty & Ensemble*
11 'That Old Church Bell' *Jo & Commodore*
12 'I Never Knew' *Jo & Ensemble*
13 'Nerves' *Dicky, Commodore & Potter*
14 Finale *Company & Ensemble*

ACT III
15 'Rally Around' *Mr. Potter & Ensemble*
16 'Run Away' *Jo & Ensemble*
17 'Our Little Desert Isle' *Mr. Potter, Commodore & Lord Glenochtie*
18 'If You Could Read My Mind' *Jo & Potter*
19 Finale

Published lyrics by PGW:
Anytime is Dancing Time
Desert Island
Honeymoon Island
I Never Knew
I'm Going to Settle Down
In Our Little Paradise
Isn't It Wonderful
It Doesn't Matter
Love's a Very Funny Thing
Lover's Quarrels
Mother Paris
Nerves!
See You Later, Girls
See You Later, Shimmy
The Train That Leaves for Town
You Whispered It
Young Man

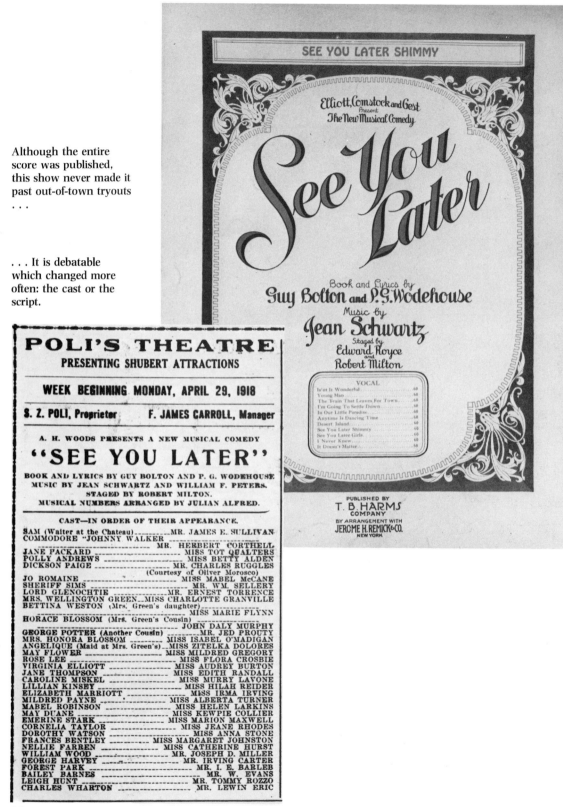

Although the entire score was published, this show never made it past out-of-town tryouts . . .

. . . It is debatable which changed more often: the cast or the script.

SEE YOU LATER SHIMMY

Elliott, Comstock and Gest
Present
The New Musical Comedy

See You Later

Book and Lyrics by
Guy Bolton and P.G. Wodehouse
Music by
Jean Schwartz
Staged by
Edward Royce
and
Robert Milton

VOCAL

Is'nt It Wonderful	.60
Young Man	.60
The Train That Leaves For Town	.60
I'm Going To Settle Down	.60
In Our Little Paradise	.60
Anytime Is Dancing Time	.60
Desert Island	.60
See You Later Shimmy	.60
See You Later Girls	.60
I Never Knew	.60
It Doesn't Matter	.60

PUBLISHED BY
T. B. HARMS
COMPANY
BY ARRANGEMENT WITH
JEROME H. REMICK & CO.
NEW YORK

POLI'S THEATRE
PRESENTING SHUBERT ATTRACTIONS

WEEK BEGINNING MONDAY, APRIL 29, 1918

S. Z. POLI, Proprietor   F. JAMES CARROLL, Manager

A. H. WOODS PRESENTS A NEW MUSICAL COMEDY

"SEE YOU LATER"

BOOK AND LYRICS BY GUY BOLTON AND P. G. WODEHOUSE
MUSIC BY JEAN SCHWARTZ AND WILLIAM F. PETERS.
STAGED BY ROBERT MILTON.
MUSICAL NUMBERS ARRANGED BY JULIAN ALFRED.

CAST—IN ORDER OF THEIR APPEARANCE.

SAM (Walter at the Chateau) _____ MR. JAMES E. SULLIVAN
COMMODORE "JOHNNY WALKER" _____
                                   MR. HERBERT CORTHELL
JANE PACKARD _____ MISS TOT QUALTERS
POLLY ANDREWS _____ MISS BETTY ALDEN
DICKSON PAIGE _____ MR. CHARLES RUGGLES
                         (Courtesy of Oliver Morosco)
JO ROMAINE _____ MISS MABEL McCANE
SHERIFF SIMS _____ MR. WM. SELLERY
LORD GLENOCHTIE _____ MR. ERNEST TORRENCE
MRS. WELLINGTON GREEN _ MISS CHARLOTTE GRANVILLE
BETTINA WESTON (Mrs. Green's daughter) _____
                                   MISS MARIE FLYNN
HORACE BLOSSOM (Mrs. Green's Cousin) _____
                                   JOHN DALY MURPHY
GEORGE POTTER (Another Cousin) _____ MR. JED PROUTY
MRS. HONORA BLOSSOM _____ MISS ISABEL O'MADIGAN
ANGELIQUE (Maid at Mrs. Green's) _ MISS ZITELKA DOLORES
MAY FLOWER _____ MISS MILDRED GREGORY
ROSE LEE _____ MISS FLORA CROSBIE
VIRGINIA ELLIOTT _____ MISS AUDREY BURTON
JANE THOMPSON _____ MISS EDITH RANDALL
CAROLINE MISKEL _____ MISS MURRY LAVONE
LILLIAN KINSEY _____ MISS HILAH REIDER
ELIZABETH MARRIOTT _____ MISS IRMA IRVING
MILDRED PAYNE _____ MISS ALBERTA TURNER
MABEL ROBINSON _____ MISS HELEN LARKINS
MAY DUANE _____ MISS KEWPIE COLLIER
EMERINE STARK _____ MISS MARION MAXWELL
CORNELIA TAYLOR _____ MISS JEANE RHODES
DOROTHY WATSON _____ MISS ANNA STONE
FRANCES BENTLEY _____ MISS MARGARET JOHNSTON
NELLIE FARREN _____ MISS CATHERINE HURST
WILLIAM WOOD _____ MR. JOSEPH D. MILLER
GEORGE HARVEY _____ MR. IRVING CARTER
FOREST PARK _____ MR. I. E. BARLEB
BAILEY BARNES _____ MR. W. EVANS
LEIGH HUNT _____ MR. TOMMY ROZZO
CHARLES WHARTON _____ MR. LEWIN ERIC

The Girl Behind The Gun

The only PGW show to recognize the First World War.

But when it came to London, it was a smash hit, with a new name and a powerful cast.

The Girl Behind the Gun

16 September 1918 (160 performances)
New Amsterdam Theatre, New York

Producers: Klaw and Erlanger
Book: Guy Bolton and P.G. Wodehouse (founded on 'Madam and her Godson' by Maurice Hennequin and Pierre Veber)
Music: Ivan Caryll
Lyrics: P.G. Wodehouse
Director: Edgar MacGregor
Choreographer: Julian Mitchell
Scenery: Clifford Pember

Cast

Robert Lambrissac	DONALD BRIAN
Pierre Breval	JOHN E. HAZZARD
Georgette Breval	ADA MEADE
Colonel Servan	FRANK DOANE
Lucienne Lambrissac	WILDA BENNETT
Harper Wentworth	BERT GARDNER
Eileen Moore	EVA FRANCIS
Brichoux	JOHN E. YOUNG
Zellie	VIRGINIA O'BRIEN

Act I   Garden of Georgette's villa, Fontainebleu
Act II   Porch of Georgette's house
Act III   Interior of Pavillion

Musical Numbers:
ACT I
1 Opening Chorus
2 'Godsons and Godmothers' *Georgette & Chorus*
3 'True to Me' *Brichoux & American girls*
4 'Happy Family' *Servan, Georgette & Lambrissac*
5 'Some Day Waiting Will End' *Lucienne & Girls*
6 'I Like It' *Breval, Lambrissac, Servan & Georgette*
7 Ensemble
ACT II
8 Opening Chorus
9 'How Warm It Is Today' *Lambrissac, Servan & Georgette*
10 'The Girl Behind the Gun' *Lucienne & Chorus*
11 'Women Haven't Any Mercy on a Man' *Breval*
12 'Life in the Old Dog Yet' *Lambrissac & Lucienne*
13 Finale – 'Flags of Allies' *Tout Ensemble*
ACT III
14 Opening Chorus
15 'Back to the Dear Old Trenches' *Lambrissac, Breval & Brichoux*

Kissing Time

20 may 1919 (430 performances)
Winter Garden Theatre, London

Producers: George Grossmith and Edward Laurillard
Musical Director: Willy Redstone

Cast

Captain Wentworth	STANLEY HOLLOWAY
Georgette St. Pol	YVONNE ARNAUD
Lady Mercia Merivale	ISOBEL JEANS
Zelie	AVICE KELHAM
Bibi St. Pol	LESLIE HENSON
Brichoux	GEORGE BARRETT
Max Touquet	GEORGE GROSSMITH
Lucienne Touquet	PHYLLIS DARE
Col. Bolinger	TOM WALLS

Lyrics published in vocal score by PGW:
Godmothers
Here's Another Godson, Girls
I've Just Come Back From Paris
Some Day, Never Forget
Wouldn't You Like Us All To Help You?

16 'There's a Light in Your Eyes' *Lambrissac & Lucienne*
17 Finale

Published lyrics by PGW:
Back to the Dear Old Trenches
The Girl Behind the Man Behind the Gun
A Happy Family
I Like It, I Like It
I've a System
Oh, How Warm It Is Today
Some Day Waiting Will End
There's a Light in Your Eyes
There's Life in the Old Dog Yet
Women Haven't Any Mercy on a Man

Kissing Time

M.H.Lawrence.

IVAN CARYLL

CHAPPELL

Ivan Caryll.

The cast of *Kissing Time*
at the Winter Garden.

PGW contributed four lyrics to this production.

The Canary

4 November 1918 (152 performances)
Globe Theatre, New York

Producer: Charles Dillingham
Music: Ivan Caryll, Irving Berlin and others
Lyrics: Anne Caldwell, P.G. Wodehouse
Directors: Fred G. Latham and Edward Royce
Scenery: Joseph Urban
Musical Director: Harold Vicars

Cast

Eugenie	DORIS FAITHFUL
Mrs. Beasley	EDNA BATES
Ned Randolph	SAM HARDY
Mr. Trimmer	GEORGE E. MACK
Dr. Dippy	LOUIS HARRISON
Dodge	JAMES DOYLE
Fleece	HARLAND DIXON
Timothy	JOSEPH CAWTHORNE
Julie	JULIA SANDERSON
Rico	WILMER BENTLEY
Mary Ellen	MAUDE EBURNE
A Minister	GEORGE EGAN

Act I   Trimmer's Antique Shop
Act II   Dr. Dippy's Sanatorium
Act III Ned's Party

Published lyrics by PGW:
The Hunting Honeymoon
Julie and Her Johnnies
That's What Men Are For
Thousands of Years Ago

Oh, My Dear!

27 November 1918 (189 performances)
Princess Theatre, New York

Producers: F. Ray Comstock and William Elliott
Book: Guy Bolton and P.G. Wodehouse
Music: Louis A. Hirsch
Lyrics: P.G. Wodehouse
Directors: Robert Milton and Edward Royce
Musical Director: Max Hirshfield

Cast

Hazel	EVELYN DORN
Dr. Rockett	FREDERICK GRAHAM
Broadway Willie Burbank	ROY ATWELL
Grace Spelvin	MARJORIE BENTLEY
Bagshott	JOSEPH ALLEN
Bruce Allenby	JOSEPH SANTLEY
Hilda Rockett	IVY SAWYER
Georgie Van Alstyne	HELEN BARNES
Pickles	MIRIAM COLLINS
Babe	HELEN CLARKE
Mrs. Rockett	GEORGIA CAINE
Jennie Wren	JULIETTE DAY
Joe Plummer	FRANCIS X. CONLAN
Nan Hatton	FLORENCE McGUIRE

Act I An open portico at the Rockett Health Farm. Afternoon

Act II Scene 1 – In front of the portico. Night
Scene 2 – Same. Early Morning

Musical Numbers:

ACT I
1 'I Shall Be All Right Now' *Willie & Girls*
2 'I Wonder Whether' *Bruce & Hilda*
3 'Ask Dad' *Georgie, Willie, Pop, Pickles & Babe*
4 'Our City of Dreams' *Hilda & Girls*
5 'Come Where Nature Calls' *Mrs. Rockett, Bruce, Hilda, Pop & Girls*
6 'Phoebe Snow' *Jennie & Girls*
7 Finale
ACT II Scene 1
8 Opening 'Go Little Boat' *Hilda, Boys & Girls*
9 'You Never Know' *Bruce, Hilda, Grace, Girls & Boys*
10 'Try Again' *Bruce, Hilda & Jennie*
11 'It Sort of Makes a Fellow Stop and Think' *Willie*
12 'Childhood Days' *Bruce, Pop, Bagshott, Georgie, Babe & Pickles*
13 Finaletto
ACT II Scene 2
14 'I'd Ask No More' *Hilda, Jennie & Boys*
15 'If They Ever Parted Me From You' *Willie & Jennie*
16 Finale

Published lyrics by PGW:
Boat Song
Childhood Days
City of Dreams
Come Where Nature Calls
I Shall Be All Right Now
I Wonder Whether I've Loved You All My Life
I'd Ask No More
If They Ever Parted You From Me
It Sorta Makes a Fellow Stop and Think
The Land Where Journeys End and Dreams Come True
You Never Know

The next Princess show, with music by Louis Hirsch and featuring comedian Roy Atwell.

Its original title was *Ask Dad.*

72

THE PLAY PICTORIAL

"THE BEAUTY PRIZE"

NO. 262

VOL. XLIV.

1S. NET

MONTHLY

MISS DOROTHY DICKSON

The above photograph in colours is supplied on thick art paper suitable for framing, price 6d.

PLAY

"THE CABARET GIRL."

VOL. XLI

1S. NET

MONTHLY

This Journal is supplied to the Trade on terms which do not allow of any discount on the published price.

A DAMSEL IN DISTRESS

BAA BAA, BLACK SHEEP

NEW THEATRE ST. MARTIN'S LANE

The Rose of China

25 November 1919 (47 performances)
Lyric Theatre, New York

Producers: F. Ray Comstock and Morris Gest
Book: Guy Bolton (based on Samuel Shipman's play
   East is West)
Music: Armand Vecsey
Lyrics: P.G. Wodehouse
Directors: Robert Milton and Julian Mitchell
Scenery: Joseph Urban
Musical Director: Frank Tours

Cast

Dum Tong, gardener	PAUL IRVING
Ton Ka, a Chinese dancer	LOUISE BROWNEL
Ling Tao	JANE RICHARDSON
Ting-Fang-Lee	STANLEY RIDGES
Tsao Ling	WILLIAM H. PRINGLE
Tommy Tilford	OSCAR SHAW
Wilson Peters	FRANK McINTYRE
Polly Baldwin	CECIL CUNNINGHAM
Priest	LEO DWYER
Chung, Tommy's servant	THOS. E. JACKSON
Grace Hobson	CYNTHIA PEROT
Mrs. Hobson, her mother	EDNA MAY OLIVER

Act I   The Garden of Tsao Ling
Act II   Tommy Tilford's Bungalow
Act III   The Terrace outside the Bungalow

Musical Numbers:

ACT I
1 Opening
   (a) Sunrise Intermezzo
   (b) Hymn to the Sun *Ensemble*
   (c) Dance *Ton Ka & Girls*
2 'Yale' *Ting-Fang-Lee & Girls*
3 'Bunny Dear' *Ling Tao & Girls*
4 'The Legend of the Tea Tree' *Ling Tao & Tommy*
5 'College Spirit' *Tommy, Wilson & Ting-Fang-Lee*
6 'What! What! What!' *Polly & Tommy*
7 Finale *Company*
ACT II
8 'Little Bride' *Ling Tao & Ensemble*
9 'Our Chinese Bungalow' *Ling Tao & Tommy*
10 'Proposals' *Polly, Wilson & Tommy*
11 'When You Are In China' *Ling Tao, Tommy,*
   Grace & Mrs. Hobson

Not quite a Princess show, even though it used the
same production team.

12 'Yesterday' *Ling Tao & Tommy*
13 Finale *Company*
ACT III
14 'Spirit of the Drum' *Ton Ka & Girls*
15 'Banks of the Subway' *Polly & Wilson*
16 'My China Rose' *Tommy & Girls*
17 'Broken Blossoms' *Ling Tao*
18 Finale *Company*

Published lyrics by PGW:
Bunny Dear
College Spirit
Down on the Banks of the Subway
In Our Bungalow
Tao Loved His Li
Yale
Yesterday

Sally

21 December 1920 (570 performances)
New Amsterdam Theatre, New York

Producer: Florenz Ziegfeld, Jr.
Book: Guy Bolton
Music: Jerome Kern
Lyrics: Clifford Grey
Director: Edward Royce
Scenery: Joseph Urban
Musical Director: Gus Salzer

This tune commemorates the place where PGW was married.

Cast

'Pops', prop. of the Alley Inn	ALFRED P. JAMES
Rosalind Rafferty, a manicurist	MARY HAY
Sascha, violinist at the Alley Inn	JACQUES RABIROFF
Otis Hooper, a theatrical agent	WALTER CATLETT
Mrs. Ten Broek, a settlement worker	DOLORES
Sally of the Alley, a foundling	MARILYNN MILLER
Connie, a waiter	LEON ERROL
Miss New York, a niece	AGATHA DEBUSSY
The Admiral Travers, a gay one	PHIL RYLEY
Blair Farquar, an only son	IRVING FISHER
Jimmie Spelvin	STANLEY RIDGES
Richard Farquar	FRANK KINGDON
Billy Porter	CARL ROSE
Harry Burton	JACK BARKER

Act I   The Alley Inn. New York
Act II   The Garden of Richard Farquar, Long Island
Act III   Scene 1 – The Land of Butterflies in the Ziegfeld Follies
Scene 2 – Sally's dressing room at the Amsterdam Theatre after the Follies première
Scene 3 – The Little Church Around the Corner

Published lyrics by PGW:
The Church Round the Corner
You Can't Keep a Good Girl Down

Dorothy Dickson, George Grossmith, and Heather Thatcher.

75

Sally

10 September 1921 (383 performances)
Winter Garden Theatre, London

Producer: George Grossmith
Director: Charles A. Maynard
Choreography: Jack Haskell
Scenery: Joseph and Phil Harker
Musical Director: John Ansell

Cast

Sascha	HERBERT FIREMAN
Jimmie Spelvin	SEYMOUR BEARD
Otis Hooper	GEORGE GROSSMITH
Rosalind Rafferty	HEATHER THATCHER
Sally of the Alley	DOROTHY DICKSON
Mrs. Ten Brock	MOLLY RAMSDEN
'Pops' Shendorff	ALARIC ARNEF
Constantine	LESLIE HENSON
Blair Farquar	GREGORY STROUD
Admiral Travers	LEIGH ELLIS
Richard Farquar	ERNEST GRAHAM
Billy Porter	JACK BRADLEY
Harry Barton	DERICK GLYNNE

Below: Leslie Henson and Dorothy Dickson. **Right: George Grossmith and Heather Thatcher.**

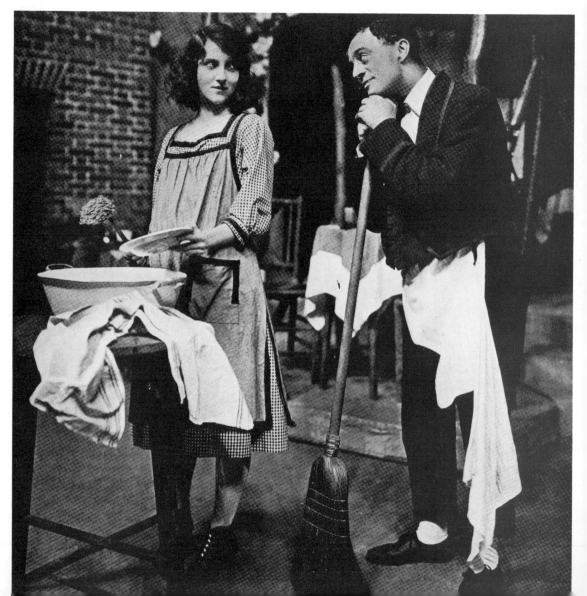

The Golden Moth

5 October 1921 (281 performances)
Adelphi Theatre, London

Producer: Austen Hurgon
Book: Fred Thompson and P.G. Wodehouse
Music: Ivor Novello
Lyrics: P.G. Wodehouse
Musical Director: Ernest Longstaffe

Cast

Pierre Caravan ('The Blackbird')	ROBERT MICHAELIS	
Dipper Tigg ('The Marquis')	W.H. BERRY	
Capt. Paul D'Artois	THORPE BATES	
Armand Bercy	FRED MAGUIRE	
Gallipaux	MOSTYN GODFREY	
Major Podoritza	MARSTON GARSIA	
Dupont	BOBBIE COMBER	
Waiter	HENRY CHANNON	
Sergeant	W.E. STEPHENS	
Corporal	LIONEL BROOKE	
Henri	AUSTIN CAMP	
Giuseppe Palata	ELLIS WILLIAMS	
Butcher Bertrand	DENHAM CHARLES	
Stranger of Marseilles	PARKER SCOTT	
Horrible Harry	M. NOEL	
Alonzo, the Assassin	HERBERT FENWICK	
The Gasper King	ANDREW JONES	
Aline	NANCE LOVAT	
Rose	CICELY DEBENHAM	
Zozo	SYLVIA LESLIE	
Simone	BARBARA ROBERTS	
Madame Dupont	MARY EWIN	

Musical Numbers:

ACT I
'We've Had a Busy Day' *Ensemble*
'Fairy Prince' *Aline & Men*
'Give Me a Thought Now and Then' *Aline & D'Artois*
'Lonely Soldier' *Rose & Chorus*
'Romance is Calling' *Aline & Blackbird*
'Dartmoor Days' *Marquis*
'Dear Eyes That Shine' *D'Artois*
Finale

ACT II
'My Girl' *Blackbird*
'Gathering Nuts in May' *Rose & Chorus*
'If I Lost You' *Rose & Marquis*

ACT III
'The Island of Never-Mind-Where' *Marquis & Chorus*
Finale

Act I   Estaminet on the de Crillon Estate, near Paris

Act II 'The Golden Moth', a crooks' rendezvous in Paris

Act III M. de Crillon's Château

Ivor Novello.

The Winter Garden Theatre, home of George
Grossmith's musicals.

The Cabaret Girl

19 September 1922 (462 performances)
Winter Garden Theatre, London

Producer: George Grossmith
Book: George Grossmith and P.G. Wodehouse
Music: Jerome Kern
Lyrics: George Grossmith and P.G. Wodehouse;
    Anne Caldwell
Choreographer: Jack Haskell
Musical Director: John Ansell

Cast

Marchioness of Harrogate	MISS FORTESCUE
Marquis of Harrogate, her son	FRED LESLIE
Effie Dix	VERA LENNOX
Commissionaire	JACK GLYNN
A Customer	DOROTHY BENTHAM
Mr. Gripps	GEORGE GROSSMITH
Mr. Gravvins	NORMAN GRIFFIN
James Paradene	GEOFFREY GWYTHER
Harry Zona	THOMAS WEGUELIN
March	SEYMOUR BEARD
April	ENID TAYLOR
Little Ada	HEATHER THATCHER
Lily de Jigger	MOLLY RAMSDEN
Marilynn Morgan ('Flick')	DOROTHY DICKSON
Feloosi, an agent	JOSEPH SPREE
Quibb, a piano tuner	LEIGH ELLIS
Mrs. Drawbridge, housekeeper	MURIEL BARNBY
The Mayor of Woollam Chersey	CLAUDE HORTON
Laburnum Brown	MOLLY VERE
Lilac Smith	VERA KIRKWOOD
Poppy Robinson	DOROTHY DEANE
Hyacinth Green	MONICA NOYES
Tulip Williams	BETTY SHIELDS
The Vicar of Woollam Chersey	ERNEST GRAHAM
Box Office Keeper	FRED WHITLOCK
Cabaret Dancer	JINOS

Act I   The Showroom of Messrs. Gripps & Gravvins,
        music publishers, Bond Street
Act II The Pergola, Woollam Chersey
Act III Scene 1 – Entrance to the 'All Night Follies'
        Scene 2 – The Cabaret

The first musical to deal with this new source of
entertainment: cabarets. It was written by PGW and
GG, and in the Grossmith tradition, was a vehicle for
the latter. GG with Norman Griffin.

Musical Numbers:
ACT I
1 'Chopin ad lib' *Girls*
2 'You Want the Best Seats, We Have 'Em' *Effie &
    Shop Girls*
3 'Mr. Gravvins-Mr. Gripps' *Gravvin & Gripps*
4 'First Rose of Summer' *Jim*
5 'Journey's End' *Marilynn & Jim*
6 'Whoop-De-Oodle-Do' *Gravvins & Cabaret Troupe*
7 'At the Ball' *Quibb*
8 'Dancing Time' *Marilynn & Gripps*
9 Finaletto *Company*
ACT II
10 'The Pergola Patrol' *Dorothy, Tradesmen, Girls*
11 'Entrance Scena' *Porters, Marilynn & Jim*
12 'Shimmy With Me' *Marilynn & Girls*
13 'Those Days Are Gone Forever' *Gravvins*
14 'Looking All Over For You' *Marilynn & Jim*
15 'Nerves' *Ada, Gripps & Gravvins*
16 Finale
ACT III
17 Opening Music
18 'London, Dear Old London' *Jim & Men*
19 Opening Music: Tango & Fox Trot
20 'Ka-Lu-A' *Marilynn & Girls*
21 'Oriental Dreams' *Company*

Published lyrics by PGW:
Vocal Score
Journey's End
Looking All Over

The Beauty Prize

5 September 1923 (214 performances)
Winter Garden Theatre, London

Producer: George Grossmith
Book: George Grossmith and P.G. Wodehouse
Music: Jerome Kern
Lyrics: George Grossmith and P.G. Wodehouse
Director: Charles A. Maynard
Choreographer: Fred A. Leslie
Musical Director: John Ansell

Cast

Hon. Dud Wellington	PETER HADDON
Meadow Grahame	DOROTHY FIELD
Mrs. Hexal	SHEILA COURTENAY
Shinny Fane	MARJORIE SPIERS
Gypsy Lorrimole	DOROTHY HURST
Flutey Warboy	GEORGE GROSSMITH
John Brooke	JACK HOBBS
Manicure Girl	KOOKOO DUNCAN
Shoe Girl	MONICA NOYES
Lingerie Girl	PHYLLIS GARTON
Hairdresser	DOROTHY DEANE
Flower Girl	MIGNON MORENZA
Dressmaker Girl	BERYL MURRAY
Glove Girl	MINETTE CORDAY
Parasol Girl	PHYLLIS SWINBURNE
Doreen	EILEEN SEYMOUR
Hector	ERNEST GRAHAM
Kitty Wren	VERA LENNOX
Carol Stuart	DOROTHY DICKSON
Lovey Toots	HEATHER THATCHER
Jones	CLAUDE HORTON
Mr. Odo Philpotts	LESLIE HENSON
Quartermaster	LEIGH ELLIS
James K. Stuart	ARTHUR FINN
Pedro	WILLIAM PARNIS
Servant	FRED WHITLOCK
Marconi Boy	WINIFRED SHOTTER
Steward	JACK GLYNN

Musical Numbers:

ACT I
Opening *Kitty, Maids & Midinettes*
'Honeymoon Isle' *Carol*
'I'm a Prize' *Carol & Odo*
'It's a Long Long Day' *Flutey*
'Joy Bells' *Sextette*

ACT II
'Mah-Jong' *Carol & Flutey*
'You Can't Make Love by Wireless' *Carol & Flutey*
'Non-Stop Dancing' *Odo & Chorus*
'For the Man I Love' *Carol & John*
'A Cottage in Kent' *Lovey & Odo*

ACT III
'Meet Me Down on Main Street' *Flutey & Odo*
'Moon Love' *Carol*
Finale

Published lyrics by PGW:

Honeymoon Isle
I'm a Prize
It's a Long Long Day
Meet Me Down on Main Street
Moon Love
Non-Stop Dancing
You Can't Make Love By Wireless

Act 1   Scene 1 – A Private Supper room at Carl's Club
Scene 2 – The Drawing room at Palace House, Kensington
Act II   The Chinese Garden Lounge on board the 'Majestania'
Act III   The Garden of James Stuart's house at Palm Beach, Florida

Heather Thatcher and Leslie Henson in *The Cabaret Girl*'s successor, which featured the Grossmith repertory company.

Dorothy Dickson and George Grossmith.

Sitting Pretty

A YEAR FROM TODAY

COMSTOCK & GEST
PRODUCE THE NEW MUSICAL COMEDY

Sitting Pretty

by BOLTON, WODEHOUSE & KERN

The last of the B-W-K efforts, this had a strong book that PGW adapted for his novel *Bill the Conqueror*.

8 April 1924 (95 performances)
Fulton Theatre, New York

Producers: F. Ray Comstock and Morris Gest
Book: Guy Bolton and P.G. Wodehouse
Music: Jerome Kern
Lyrics: P.G. Wodehouse
Directors: Fred G. Latham and Julian Alfred
Musical Director: Max Steiner

Cast

Mrs. Wagstaff, a teacher	MARJORIE EGGLESTON
James, a footman	ALBERT WYART
Roper, a butler	HARRY LILFORD
'Bill' Pennington	RUDOLPH CAMERON
Judson Waters, his friend	EUGENE REVERE
Babe LaMarr, a chorus girl	MYRA HAMPTON
May Tolliver	GERTRUDE BRYAN
Dixie, her sister	QUEENIE SMITH (courtesy of Wilmer & Vincent)
Jasper	EDWARD FINLEY
Wilhelmina	JAYNE CHESNEY
Otis	GEORGE SYLVESTER
Wilhelmina	MARIAN DICKSON
Mr. Pennington	GEORGE E. MACK
Horace	DWIGHT FRYE
Joe, his uncle	FRANK McINTYRE
Bolt, a coachman	GEORGE O'DONNELL
Jane, a housemaid	TERRY BLAINE
Prof. Appleby	GEORGE SPELVIN

Act I Garden of Mr. Pennington's summer house at Far Hills, New Jersey
Act II Patio of Mr. Pennington's winter home at Belleair, Florida

Sitting Pretty stars: PGW in centre, flanked on the left by Queenie Smith, on the right by Gertrude Bryan, all sitting very pretty at this point in their careers.

Musical Numbers:
ACT I
The Charity Class *Charity Girls*
'Is This Not a Lovely Spot' *Pennington, Bill, Judson, Girls*
'Worries' *May, Dixie & Bill*
'Mr. & Mrs. Rorer' *Dixie, Horace & Cooking Class*
'Bongo on the Congo' *Horace, Judson & Uncle Joe*
'There Isn't One Girl' *Bill, Roper & May*
'A Year From Today' *Bill & May*
'Shufflin' Sam' *Dixie & Ensemble*
Finaletto *Ensemble*
ACT II
'The Polka Dot' *Ensemble*
'Days Gone By' *Dorothy Janice & Ensemble*
'All You Need is a Girl' *Bill & May*
'Dear Old Fashioned Prison of Mine' *Horace & Uncle Joe*
'A Desert Island' *May, Dixie & Girls*
'The Magic Train' *Bill, May & Ensemble*
'Shadow of the Moon' *Dixie & Men*
'Sitting Pretty' *Horace, Dixie & Ensemble*
Finale *Ensemble*

Published lyrics by PGW:
All You Need is a Girl
Bongo on the Congo
The Enchanted Train
Mr. & Mrs. Rorer
On a Desert Island With You
Shadow of the Moon
Shufflin' Sam
Sitting Pretty
Tulip Time in Sing Sing
Worries
A Year From Today

The star of *Sitting Pretty*.

Best wishes to gladys from Queenie Smith

86

ACT TWO

'Before Larry Hart, only P.G. Wodehouse had made any assault on the intelligence of the song-listening public.'
RICHARD RODGERS

This is the trio of musical fame
    Bolton and Wodehouse and Kern.
Better than anyone else you can name,
    Bolton and Wodehouse and Kern.
Nobody knows what on earth they've been bitten by:
All I can say is I mean to get lit an' buy
Orchestra seats for the next one that's written by
    Bolton and Wodehouse and Kern.

Hearts and Diamonds

1 June 1926 (46 performances)
Strand Theatre, London

Producer: Arthur Bourchier
Book: Ernst Marischka and Bruno Granichstadten
(from 'The Orlov')
English Adaptation: P.G. Wodehouse and Laurie Wylie
Music: Bruno Granischstadten and Max Darewski
Lyrics: Graham John
Director, Scenic Designer and Costumer: Theodore
Komisarjevsky
Choreography: Edward Dolly

Cast

Hunter	J.S. CARRE
Alexander Dorotchinsky	GEORGE METAXA
John Walsh	CHARLES STONE
Jefferson	LUPINO LANE
Mildred Harris	DARLY AITKEN
Gladys Fayne	DOROTHY DAW
Dolly Watchett	ANITA ELSON
Nadya Nadyakovska	LOUISE EDVINA
A Typist	LALA COLLINS
Purvis (Walsh's butler)	COLIN JOHNSTON
A Stranger	WALLACE LUPINO
Inspector Collins	ERIC ROLAND
Stepanov	WILFRID CAITHNESS
Myra Clay	ENA EVANS
Esme Symes	KATHLEEN CARROLL
Douglas Roach	C. O'HARA
Victor	HARRY HILLIARD

Act I   Interior of Walsh-Jefferson Motor Works
Act II   Garden fete at Walsh House
Act III   At 'The Scarlet Circle' night club

**Famed Theodore Komisarjevsky, making his West
End directorial debut.**

The Play's the Thing

3 November 1926 (326 performances)
Henry Miller's Theatre, New York

Producer: Gilbert Miller
Play: P.G. Wodehouse (adapted from the Hungarian
   of Ferenc Molnar)
Director: Gilbert Miller

Cast

Sandor Turai	HOLBROOK BLINN
Mansky	HUBERT DRUCE
Albert Adam	EDWARD CRANDALL
Ilona Szabo	CATHERINE DALE OWEN
Almady	REGINALD OWEN
Johann Dwornitschek	RALPH NAIRN
Mell	CLAUDE ALLISTER
Lackeys	STEPHEN KENDAL
	and JOHN GERARD

The action takes place in a room in a castle on the Italian
Riviera on a Saturday in summer.

Act I   2:00 a.m.
Act II   6:00 a.m.
Act III 7:30 p.m.

**Left to right: Hubert Druce, John Gerard, Edward
Crandall, Catherine Dale Owen, Claude Allister,
Reginald Owen, Stephen Kendal and Holbrook
Blinn.**

The Play's the Thing

4 December 1928
St. James's Theatre, London

Producers: Gerald du Maurier and Gilbert Miller
Director: Gerald du Maurier

Cast
Mansky   EDMOND BREON
Sandor Turai   GERALD DU MAURIER
Albert Adam   HENRY FORBES-
                                 ROBERTSON
Johann Dwornitschek   RALPH NAIRN
Almady   HENRY DANIELL
Ilona Szabo   URSULA JEANS
Mell   LAWRENCE HANRAY
Two Lackeys   JOHN CHEATLE
                                 and DENIS MANTELL

PGW's adaptation became a comedy classic.

The Play's the Thing

28 April 1948 (244 performances)
Booth Theatre, New York

Producers: Gilbert Miller, James Russo and Michael Ellis
Director: Gilbert Miller
Lighting: Ralph Alswang
Scenery: Oliver Messel

Cast
Sandor Turai   LOUIS CALHERN
Mansky   ERNEST COSSART
Albert Adam   RICHARD HYLTON
Johann Dwornitschek   FRANCIS COMPTON
Ilona Szabo   FAYE EMERSON
Almady   ARTHUR MARGETSON
Mell   CLAUDE ALLISTER
Lackeys   TED PATERSON
                                 and FRED WENTLER

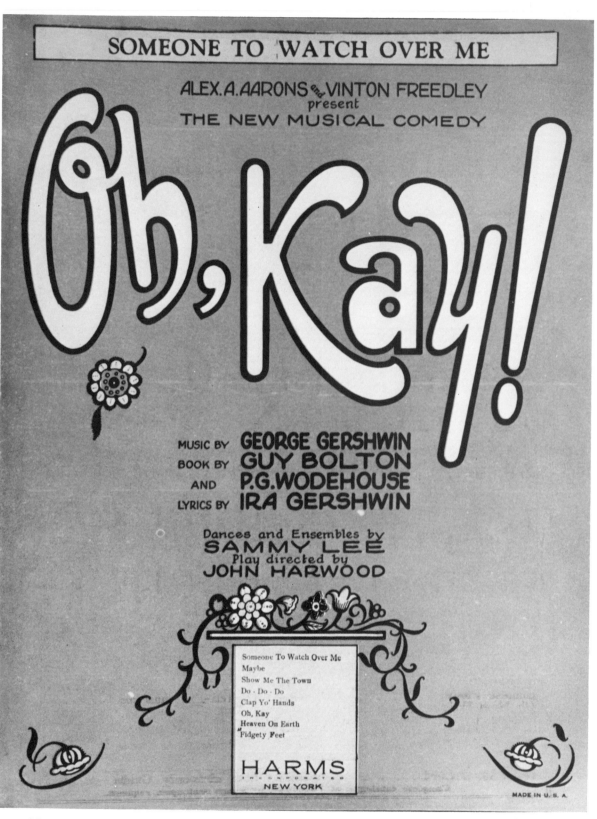

Oh, Kay!

8 November 1926 (256 performances)
Imperial Theatre, New York

Producers: Alex A. Aarons and Vinton Freedley
Book: Guy Bolton and P.G. Wodehouse
Music: George Gershwin
Lyrics: Ira Gershwin
Director: John Harwood
Choreography: Sammy Lee
Scenery: John Wenger
Musical Director: William Daly
Duo-Pianists: Victor Arden and Phil Ohman

Cast

Molly Morse	BETTY COMPTON
Peggy	JANETTE GILMORE
The Duke	GERALD OLIVER SMITH
Larry Potter	HARLAND DIXON
Phil Ruxton	MARION FAIRBANKS
Dolly Ruxton	MADELEINE FAIRBANKS
'Shorty' McGee	VICTOR MOORE
Constance Appleton	SASCHA BEAUMONT
Jimmy Winter	OSCAR SHAW
Kay	GERTRUDE LAWRENCE
Revenue Officer Jansen	HARRY T. SHANNON
Mae	CONSTANCE CARPENTER
Daisy	PAULETTE WINSTON
Judge Appleton	FRANK GARDINER

Place – Beachampton, Long Island
Act I   Scene 1 – Living Hall of Jimmy's house
         Scene 2 – Same. Next Morning
Act II   Scene 1 – Terrace of Jimmy's house
         Scene 2 – The Cellar
         Scene 3 – Indian Inlet Inn

Left: Bolton and PGW's strong book and the Gershwin brothers' score were responsible for this 1926 masterpiece of prohibition.

Above: PGW discusses plot with Gertrude Lawrence, star of the English production.

Oh, Kay!

21 September 1927 (213 performances)
His Majesty's Theatre, London

Director: William Ritter
Choreographer: Elsie Neal
Musical Director: Arthur Wood

Cast

Molly	RITA McLEAN
Peggy	CECILE MAULE-COLE
Dolly Ruxton	BETH DODGE
Phillipa Ruxton	BETTY DODGE
Larry Potter	ERIC COXON
The Duke of Datchet	CLAUDE HULBERT
Revenue Officer Jansen	PERCY PARSONS
Chauffeur	JACK DALMAYNE
Jimmy Winter	HAROLD FRENCH
Constance Appleton	APRIL HARMON
'Shorty' McGee	JOHN KIRBY
Kay	GERTRUDE LAWRENCE
Judge Appleton	CHARLES CAUTLEY
Daisy	PHYLLIS DAWN

ALEX. A. AARONS and VINTON FREEDLEY
Present
THE NEW MUSICAL COMEDY

Oh, Kay!

—with—

GERTRÚDE LAWRENCE   OSCAR SHAW
VICTOR MOORE

Book by Guy Bolton and P. G. Wodehouse
Music by George Gershwin
Lyrics by Ira Gershwin
Book Staged by John Harwood
Dances and Ensembles Staged by Sammy Lee
Settings Designed and Painted by John Wenger

THE CAST
(In the Order of their Appearance)

MOLLY MORSE....................BETTY COMPTON
MAE...........................CONSTANCE CARPENTER
THE DUKE..................GERALD OLIVER SMITH
LARRY POTTER....................HARLAND DIXON
PHIL BUXTON...............MARION FAIRBANKS
DOLLY RUXTON............MADELEINE FAIRBANKS
REVENUE OFFICER JANSEN......HARRY T. SHANNON
CONSTANCE APPLETON.........SASCHA BEAUMONT
JIMMY WINTER........................OSCAR SHAW
"SHORTY" McGEE....................VICTOR MOORE
KAY..........................GERTRUDE LAWRENCE
PEGGY.....................JANETTE GILMORE
DAISY.....................PAULETTE WINSTON
JUDGE APPLETON.............FRANK GARDINER
VICTOR ARDEN and PHIL OHMAN at the Pianos

LADIES OF THE ENSEMBLE
Peggy Quinn, Marie Otto, Elsie Neal, Grace Jones, May Sullivan,
Ann Ecklund, Marcia Bell, Betty Waxton, Anita Gordon,
Blanche O'Donahue, Jean Carroll, Frances Stone, Maxine Mar-
shall, Elsie Frank, Amy Frank, Dorothy Saunders, Amy Weber-
Kappie Fay, Bonnie Blackwood, Pansy Maness, Caroline Phillips,
Peggy Johnstone, Polly Williams, Adrienne Armond, Gloria
Murray, Grace Carroll, Betty Vane, Frances DeFoe, Winifred
Beck, Alice Monroe, Ila Roye, Mildred Brower, Ruth Savoy.

GENTLEMEN OF THE ENSEMBLE
Al Fisher, Lionel Maclyn, Jacques Stone, Tom Martin, Melville
Chapman, Alan Stevens, Ted White, Bob Gebhardt, Burton
McEvilly, Dowell Brown, Eugene Day, Sam Fischer.

'The book of Oh Kay! *was written by Guy Bolton and P.G. Wodehouse, than whom there are no better librettists writing for our stage.'*
BURNS MANTLE

Gertrude Lawrence supported by Harold French and John Kirby in *Oh, Kay!* at His Majesty's.

Oh, Kay!

16 April 1960 (89 performances)
East 74th Street Theatre, New York

Producers: Leighton K. Brill, Frederick Lewis, Jr.,
   and Bertram Yarborough
Director: Bertram Yarborough
Choreographer: Dania Krupska
Scenery: Don Jensen
Costumes: Pearl Somner
Lighting: Richard Nelson
Musical Director: Dorothea Freitag

Cast

The Cotton Tails:	
Phil	ROSEMARRI SHEER
Izzy	LINDA LAVIN
Polly	PENNY FULLER
Jean	FRANCESCA BELL
Odile	LYNN GAY LORINO
Molly	SYBIL SCOTFORD
Larry Potter	EDDIE PHILLIPS
Earl of Blandings	MURRAY MATHESON
McGee	BERNIE WEST
Chauffeur	JAMES SULLIVAN
Jimmy Winters	DAVID DANIELS
Constance	EDITH BELL
Revenue Officer	MIKE MAZURKI
Kay	MARTI STEVENS
Judge Appleton	JOSEPH MACAULAY

Songs added with lyrics by PGW:
'The Twenties Are Here to Stay'
'The Pophams'
'You'll Still Be There'

From the Off-Broadway revival.

96

The Nightingale

3 January 1927 (96 performances)
Jolson Theatre, New York

Producers: The Messrs. Shubert
Book: Guy Bolton (based on the life of Jenny Lind)
Music: Armand Vecsey
Lyrics: P.G. Wodehouse
Director: Lewis Morton
Choreographer: Carl Hemmer
Scenery: Watson Barratt
Musical Director: Alfred Goodman

Cast

Major General Gurnee	LUCIUS HENDERSON
Mrs. Gurnee	SOPHIE EVERETT
Mr. Carp	STANLEY LUPINO
Col. Wainwright	JOHN GAINES
Mrs. Vischer Van Loo	CLARA PALMER
Alice Wainwright	EILEEN VAN BIENE
Capt. Joe Archer	ROBERT HOBBS
Piper	THOMAS WHITELEY
Josephine	VIOLET CARLSON
Cadet Officer	DONALD BLACK
Jenny Lind	ELEANOR PAINTER
Whistler	HAROLD WOODWARD
Stephen Rutherford	NICHOLAS JOY
Capt. Rex Gurnee	RALPH ERROLLE
P.T. Barnum	TOM WISE
Col. Robert E. Lee	VICTOR BOZARDT
Dolly (maid)	EILEEN CARMODY
Susan (maid)	ARLINE MELBURN
Otto Goldschmidt	WILLIAM TUCKER
Signor Belletti	IVAN DNEPROFF
Butler – Rutherford's	JOHN GAINES
Footman – Rutherford's	NEAL FRANK
Usher – Castle Garden	ROBERT HARPER
Cornelius Vanderbilt	VICTOR BOZARDT

Act I   Scene 1 – The Terrace of the Old Hotel at West Point

Act II Scene 1 – Jenny Lind's bedroom in the New York Hotel. A year later
        Scene 2 – Outside the hotel
        Scene 3 – Steve Rutherford's house

Act III A year later
        Scene 1 – The lobby of Castle Garden
        Scene 2 – The stage of Castle Garden

Musical Numbers:

ACT I
Opening Chorus *Girls*
'Breakfast in Bed' *Carp, Josephine*
March song *West Pointers*
Waltz song *Jenny*
'Homeland' *Rex & Ensemble*
'May Moon' *Jenny & Rex*
'Two Little Ships' *Alice, Joe & Girls*
'He Doesn't Know' *Carp*
Finale

ACT II
'Fairyland' *Jenny, Dolly & Susan*
Trio *Belletti, Otto & Josephine*
'Santa Claus' *Carp & Piper*
'Josephine' *Carp & Josephine*
'Once in September' *Rex & Alice*

ACT III
'Breakfast in Bed' *Carp & Josephine*
'Comin' Thru the Rye' *Jenny*
Finale

Published lyrics by PGW:
Breakfast in Bed
May Moon
Two Little Ships

Her Cardboard Lover

21 March 1927 (152 performances)
Empire Theatre, New York

Producers: Gilbert Miller and A.H. Woods
Play: Valerie Wyngate and P.G. Wodehouse (from
the French play by Jacques Deval)
Director: Gilbert Miller

Cast

Monsieur Bonnavant	ERNEST STALLARD
Charly	ARTHUR LEWIS
Paul Guisard	TERENCE NEIL
André Sallicel	LESLIE HOWARD
A Croupier	CHARLES ESDALE
Simone	JEANNE EAGELS
Cloakroom attendant	HENRY VINCENT
Tony Lagorce	STANLEY LOGAN
Albine	VALERIE WYNGATE

**PGW did the New York adaptation. The English
version starred Tallulah Bankhead with Leslie
Howard repeating his American performance.**

Act I   Bar of the Baccarat Room, Hendaye
Act II   Simone's bedroom in her Paris apartment
Act III   The same

Good Morning, Bill!

28 November 1927 (136 performances)
Duke of York's Theatre, London

Producer: Athole Stewart
Play: P.G. Wodehouse (based on the Hungarian of
 Ladislaus Fodor)
Director: Sam Lysons

Cast

Marie	BARBARA WILCOX
Lord Tidmouth	LAWRENCE GROSSMITH
Lottie	DOROTHY MINTO
Bill Paradene	ERNEST TRUEX
Bell-boy	E. HALLOWS
Sally Smith, M.D.	VERA LENNOX
Sir Hugo Drake	FRANK CELLIER

Act I   A suite in the Esplanade Hotel at Marvis
 Beach, Sussex
Acts II & III   Bill Paradene's country house in
 Hampshire

**This hilarious comedy
highlighted the
Grossmith repertory
company, with brother
Lawrence substituting
for George.**

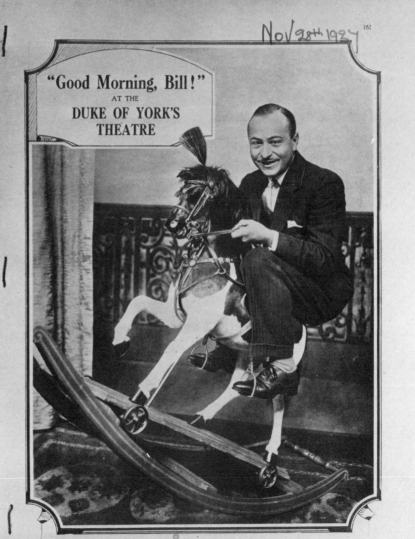

ERNEST TRUEX, WHOSE CLEVER ACTING IS A FEATURE OF THE PLAY

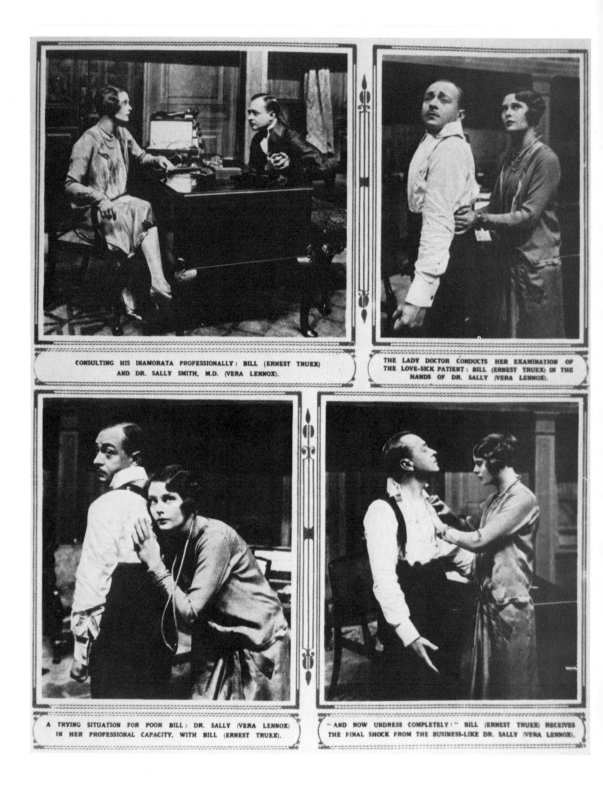

CONSULTING HIS INAMORATA PROFESSIONALLY: BILL (ERNEST TRUEX) AND DR. SALLY SMITH, M.D. (VERA LENNOX).

THE LADY DOCTOR CONDUCTS HER EXAMINATION OF THE LOVE-SICK PATIENT: BILL (ERNEST TRUEX) IN THE HANDS OF DR. SALLY (VERA LENNOX).

A TRYING SITUATION FOR POOR BILL: DR. SALLY (VERA LENNOX) IN HER PROFESSIONAL CAPACITY, WITH BILL (ERNEST TRUEX).

"AND NOW UNDRESS COMPLETELY!" BILL (ERNEST TRUEX) RECEIVES THE FINAL SHOCK FROM THE BUSINESS-LIKE DR. SALLY (VERA LENNOX).

DUKE OF YORK'S THEATRE.

"GOOD MORNING, BILL!"

By P. G. WODEHOUSE. Based on the
Hungarian of LADISLAUS FODOR.

Marie	..	.. BARBARA WILCOX
Lord Tidmouth	..	.. LAWRENCE GROSSMITH
Lottie	..	.. DOROTY MINTO
Bill Paradene	..	.. ERNEST TRUEX
Bell-Boy	..	.. E. HALLOWS
Sally Smith, M.D.	..	.. VERA LENNOX
Sir Hugo Drake	..	.. FRANK CELLIER.

How refreshing it is to laugh in a theatre with one whose humour is neither blatant, nor coarse, nor cruel ; whose silliness, when he is silly, has the good sting of character to save it, and whose scenes of nonsense have an easy, graceful good-humour which makes unnecessary in them the noisy violence that is too often the only support of farce. The truth is that Mr. Wodehouse is a stylist. He has not wit as the Restoration understood wit. He has not a great abundance, and certainly he has not beauty, of language ; a part of his humour, indeed, is the humour of the inarticulate. On the surface he appears to be no more than the teller of a thin tale which depends for its effect on a kind of felicitous inanity and a certain extravagance of speech. But he is much more than that. His follies have a form that is the very spice of folly, his twists of dialogue have a delightful unexpectedness that suddenly throws light on personality, and the whole play bears the impress of its writer's mind.

We are almost ashamed to say crudely that this is the history of Bill Paradene, who was enchanted by a distant prospect of Dr. Sally Smith on the golf links, and called her in by mistake to attend Lottie, the lady of whom he was growing tired It seems almost as unjust to add that Dr Sally and Lottie afterwards occupied two bedrooms in Bill's country house, and that, in spite of the confusions of his beauty uncle and his absurd friend, Bill succeeded at last in ridding himself of one lady and winning the other. Yet that is the whole story, and we make it sound no better if we indicate its embroideries—Dr. Sally's professional examination of the man who loved her, or Uncle Hugo's putting practice, or Lord Tidmouth's little jokes about his one umbrella and his many wives. What tedious stuff it sounds, and how tedious it would have been if Mr. Wodehouse had not written it, if it had not been lightened and shaped and illuminated by his style !

With that advantage, it is the most cheerful of entertainments. Though Miss Dorothy Minto played her part admirably, we were glad not to see too much of Lottie, for she was a little rougher than Mr. Wodehouse's best manner. The others moved with perfect ease from quiet nonsense that won a smile through more vigorous nonsense that earned its laughter to a final touch of sentiment that was a return to smiles again. Mr. Cellier played his golf with an extraordinary delicacy ; Miss Barbara Wilcox hinted at the lighter secrets of maidservants; and, as for Bill's friend, Lord Tidmouth, is there not an animal in America called the " tosh-horse " ? Mr. Lawrence Grossmith rode it with miraculous skill. Miss Vera Lennox was the lady-doctor. She conducted her examinations with a kind of twinkling abruptness that was exquisitely poised between coquetry and severity, and Mr. Ernest Truex mingled courage, humility, and ridiculous pathos so ingeniously that Bill seemed almost as lovable as he was absurd. Perhaps every one who applauded knew that the play was all about nothing, but they applauded without shame the rare delights of farcical style.

Good Morning, Bill!

20 March 1934 (78 performances)
Daly's Theatre, London

Producer: Peter Haddon
Director: Reginald Bach

Cast

Marie	MARY GODWIN
Lord Tidmouth	LAWRENCE GROSSMITH
Lottie	PHYLLIS MONKMAN
Bill Paradene	PETER HADDON
Luggage Porter	HENRY THOMAS
Sally Smith, M.D.	WINIFRED SHOTTER
Sir Hugo Drake	SEBASTIAN SMITH

Show Boat

Left: PGW's most successful song 'Bill' was originally written for *Oh Lady!Lady!!*, but was dropped on the road.

Helen Morgan made 'Bill' famous with her classic performance atop a piano.

Marie Burke rehearsing 'Bill' for the English production.

Right: leading man Jack Donahue, co-composer George Gershwin at piano, co-composer Sigmund Romberg, star Marilyn Miller, and producer Florenz Ziegfeld, Jr. at the first rehearsal of *Rosalie*.

Rosalie

10 January 1928 (335 performances)
New Amsterdam Theatre, New York

Producer: Florenz Ziegfeld, Jr.
Book: William Anthony McGuire and Guy Bolton
Music: George Gershwin and Sigmund Romberg
Lyrics: Ira Gershwin and P.G. Wodehouse
Choreographer: Seymour Felix
Scenery: Joseph Urban

Cast

Capt. Carl Rabisco	HALFORD YOUNG	Marinna	ANTONIA LALSEW
Michael O'Brien	CLARENCE OLIVER	Steward	CHARLES GOTTHOLD
Mary O'Brien	BOBBE ARNST	Corps. Lieutenant	JACK BRUNS
Prince Rabisco	A.P. KAYE	Superintendent of	CHARLES GOTTHOLD
HRH King Cyril	FRANK MORGAN	West Point	
HRH Queen	MARGARET DALE	Capt. Banner	CLAY CLEMENT
Sister Angelica	KATHERINE BURKE	Ex-King of Portugal	CHARLES DAVIS
Bill Delroy	JACK DONAHUE	Ex-King of Bulgaria	CLARENCE DE SILVA
Lieut. Richard Fay, U.S.A.	OLIVER McLENNAN	Ex-King of Prussia	HENRI JACKIN
		Ex-King of Greece	MARK SHULL
Princess Rosalie	MARILYN MILLER	Ex-King of Bavaria	HARRY DONAGHY
		Ex-King of Turkey	EDGAR WELCH

Published lyrics by PGW:
Hussars March
Oh Gee! Oh Joy!
Say So
West Point Song
Why Must We Always Be Dreaming

LYRIC THEATRE

DENNIS KING in
"THE THREE
MUSKETEERS"

DENNIS KING
VIVIENNE OSBORNE
LOUIS HECTOR

SCENES BY JOSEPH URBAN
Popular Priced Matinees Thurs & Sat.

ZIEGFELD

Outstanding Musical Triumph
Glorifying the American Theatre
A Magnificent Masterpiece
That Every One Should See

RUDOLPH FRIML'S
MOST FASCINATING MUSIC

WM. ANTHONY McGUIRE'S MUSICAL VERSION OF
ALEXANDRE DUMAS'
WORLD'S GREATEST ROMANCE

YOU CAN BUY YOUR SEATS AT BOX OFFICE
AT BOX OFFICE PRICES TO SUIT EVERY
PURSE   328 SEATS AT $1

VIVIENNE SEGAL

LESTER ALLEN

REGINALD OWEN

JOHN CLARKE

CLARENCE DERWENT

JOSEPH MACAULAY DETMAR POPPEN DOUGLAS DUMBRILLE
and YVONNE D'ARLE

ALBERTINA RASCH DANCERS - HARRIET HOCTOR

WALTER EDWARD BLYTHE

DENNIS KING

The Three Musketeers

13 March 1928 (318 performances)
Lyric Theatre, New York

Producer: Florenz Ziegfeld, Jr.
Book: William Anthony McGuire
Music: Rudolf Friml
Lyrics: P.G. Wodehouse and Clifford Grey
Director: William Anthony McGuire
Choreographers: Albertina Rasch and Richard Boleslavsky
Scenery: Joseph Urban

Cast

Sergeant Jussac	ROBERT D. BURNS
Comte De La Rochefort	LOUIS HECTOR
Innkeeper	HARRISON BROCKBANK
Zoe	NAOMI JOHNSON
Lady De Winter	VIVIENNE OSBORNE
Porthos	DETMAR POPPEN
Athos	DOUGLASS R. DUMBRILLE
Aramis	JOSEPH MACAULAY
Constance Bonacieux	VIVIENNE SEGAL
Planchet	LESTER ALLEN
D'Artagnan	DENNIS KING
Anne, Queen of France	YVONNE D'ARLE
M. De Treville	JOHN M. KLINE
The Duke of Buckingham	JOHN CLARKE
Cardinal Richelieu	REGINALD OWEN
Louix XIII	CLARENCE DERWENT
Brother Joseph	WILLIAM KERSHAW
Première Danseuse of the Court	HARRIET HOCTOR
Aubergiste	AUDREY DAVIS
The Bo'sun	JOHN MUCCIO
Patrick valet to Buckingham	NORMAN IVES
Cardinal's Guards	CHARLES SUTTON and GERALD ROGERS
The King's Attendant	GERALD MOORE

Published lyrics by PGW:
March of the Musketeers
Your Eyes

Dennis King as D'Artagnan.

The Three Musketeers

28 March 1930 (242 performances)
Drury Lane Theatre, London

Producer: Felix Edwardes
Director: Alfred Butt
Choreographer: Anatole Bourman
Musical Director: Herman Finck

Cast

Sergeant Jussac	JOHN ROBERTS
Comte de Rochefort	LOUIS HECTOR
Innkeeper	GORDON CROCKER
Zoe	MOYA NUGENT
Lady de Winter	MARIE NEY
Porthos	ROBERT WOOLLARD
Athos	JACK LIVESEY
Aramis	RAYMOND NEWELL
Constance Bonacieux	ADRIENNE BRUNE
Planchet	JERRY VERNO
D'Artagnan	DENNIS KING
Anne, Queen of France	LILIAN DAVIES
M. de Treville	STEPHEN T. EWART
The Duke of Buckingham	WEBSTER BOOTH
Cardinal Richelieu	ARTHUR WONTNER
Louix XIII	GEORGE BISHOP
Brother Joseph	ERIC J. HODGES
Première Danseuse of the Court	ULA SHARON
Aubergiste	ALINE AVERY
The Bo'sun	ERNEST LUDLOW
Patric, valet to Buckingham	WALTER WEBSTER
Cardinal's Guards	WALTER CUTLER and JOHN DELANEY
The King's Attendant	A.J. WILLARD

A Damsel in Distress

13 August 1928 (242 performances)
New Theatre, London

Producer: Nicholas Hannen
Play: Ian Hay and P.G. Wodehouse (based on
  PGW's novel)

Cast

Mac, a stagedoor keeper	REGINALD PURDEL	Alice Faraday	CELIA GLYNN
Billie Dove	ISABEL WILFORD	Reggie Higgins	HENRY KENDALL
George Bevan	BASIL FOSTER	Dr. Mossop, Dean of	PHILIP STANTON
Lady Maud Marsh	JANE BAXTER	Dumbleton	
Percy, Viscount Totleigh	REGINALD GARDINER	Mrs. Mossop	VIVIENNE WHITAKER
A Policeman	F.J. ARLTON	Lady Prudence Willowby	ANN TODD
Albert Keggs	AUBREY MATHER	Captain Plummer	GUY FLETCHER
Albertina Keggs	CLARICE HARDWICKE	Miss Mould	JOAN HICKSON
Lady Caroline Higgins	HELEN HAYE	Austen Gray	THOMAS WEGUELIN
The Earl of Marshmoreton	CLIVE CURRIE		

Act I   Scene 1 – The stage door of the Regality
            Theatre
            Scene 2 – Totleigh Castle
Act II   The same, a week later
Act III   Ye Dolly Varden Tea Shoppe, Hanover
            Square, next morning

The first and most successful of PGW's staged novels aided by Ian Hay. *Damsel* marked the beginning of the New Theatre Repertory Company's association with Wodehouse's farces. Left to right: Aubrey Mather, Helen Haye, Clive Currie, Basil Foster, Jane Baxter, Reginald Gardiner and Henry Kendall.

BREAKING INTO TUCKLEFORD VICARAGE: CHICKIE (CLARICE HARDWICKE) AND HUGO BONSOR (HENRY KENDALL) AS THE REFUGEES FROM THE RAIDED NIGHT CLUB.

AN AWKWARD MOMENT: CHICKIE (CLARICE HARDWICKE) IN CLERICAL DISGUISE ON THE VICARAGE ROOF, WHILE THE REV. AUBREY (AUBREY MATHER) ENTERTAINS THE MASQUERADING HUGO (HENRY KENDALL).

THE VICARAGE LUNCH TO THE BRIDE AND BRIDEGROOM: L. TO R., CHICKIE (CLARICE HARDWICKE) AS THE DEAN OF PAGA-PAGA, HUGO (HENRY KENDALL), OSBERT (REGINALD GARDINER), EMILY (DIANA BEAUMONT), AND MRS. POTTLE (JOAN HICKSON).

DISGUISED AS THE CLERGYMAN AND THE GARDENER'S BOY: HUGO (HENRY KENDALL) AND CHICKIE (CLARICE HARDWICKE).

THE HAY AND WODEHOUSE FARCE: "BAA, BAA, BLACK SHEEP."

Baa, Baa, Black Sheep

Left: another Hay
collaboration, this one
adapted from a Hay
novel.

22 April 1929 (115 performances)
New Theatre, London

Producer: Ian Hay
Play: Ian Hay and P.G. Wodehouse (based on a
   short story by Ian Hay)

Cast

Hugo Bonsor	HENRY KENDALL	Oenone	ANN TODD
Chickie Buff	CLARICE HARDWICKE	Geoffrey	HUGH DEMPSTER
Osbert Bassington-Bassington	REGINALD GARDINER	Sergeant Gannett	THOMAS WEGUELIN
		Sam Gannett	ALBAN BLAKELOCK
Hermia Wyndrum	JANE BAXTER	Mr. Tickle	SAM LYSONS
Aubrey Wyndrum	AUBREY MATHER	Mrs. Tickle	ELEANOR STREET
Harriet Knaggs	SONIA BELLAMY	Mrs. Pottle	JOAN HICKSON
Walpole Wyndrum	CLIVE CURRIE	Emily Pottle	DIANA BEAUMONT

Act I   Scene 1 – Chickie Buff's dressing-room
             (Night)
             Scene 2 – The Vicarage, Tuckleford (The
             next morning)
Act II   The Same (a quarter of an hour later)
Act III   The Same (an hour later)

Candle-Light

30 September 1929 (128 performances)
Empire Theatre, New York

Producer: Gilbert Miller
Play: P.G. Wodehouse (adapted from play by
   Siegfried Geyer)
Director: Gilbert Miller

Cast

Marie	GERTRUDE LAWRENCE	Baron von Rischenheim	ROBERT ENGLISH
Prince Rudolf Haseldorf-Schlobitten	REGINALD OWEN	Baroness von Rischenheim	BETTY SCHUSTER
		Liserl	RITA VALE
		A Waiter	RALPH ROBERTS
Josef, his valet	LESLIE HOWARD	Koeppke, a chauffeur	JACK CARLTON

The action takes place on a December evening, in the
Prince's apartment in Vienna.

Leave It To Psmith

The third and last of the
farces, from PGW's well-
known novel of the
same name. The 'P' is
silent as in pshrimp.

First produced April 22nd 1929

NEW THEATRE
ST. MARTIN'S LANE, W.C.2.
Licensed by the Lord Chamberlain to LADY WYNDHAM (Miss Mary Moore.)

P. G. WODEHOUSE and IAN HAY

Lessees:
THE WYNDHAM THEATRES Ltd.

Chairman
LADY WYNDHAM
(Miss Mary Moore)

Managing Directors
HOWARD WYNDHAM and
BRONSON ALBERY

Shaftesbury Theatre

Leave it to Psmith

Leave It To Psmith

27 September 1930 (156 performances)
Shaftesbury Theatre, London

Producer: Frank Cellier
Play: Ian Hay and P.G. Wodehouse (based on PGW's
    novel)

Cast

The Earl of Middlewick	CLIVE CURRIE
Bellows	ROGER MAXWELL
Freddie Bosham	REGINALD GARDINER
Rupert Baxter	EDWARD CHAPMAN
Phyllis Jackson	NONNIE TAYLOR
Lady Middlewick	EILEEN MUNRO
A Lift Man	EDWARD CHAPMAN
Cynthia McTodd	THEA HOLME
Eve Halliday	JANE BAXTER
Ronald Eustace Psmith	BASIL FOSTER
Eddie Cootes	AUBREY MATHER
Gladys Rumbelow	JOAN HICKSON
Christopher Walderwick	JOHN CHARLTON
Ralston McTodd	JACK LAMBERT
Agatha Crofton	BLANCHE ADELE
Ethelberta Fitzwiggin	KATHLEEN JAMES
Aileen Peavey	OLIVE BLAKENEY
Viscount Chipstead	ARTHUR VEZIN

Act I   Scene 1 – The Oak Gallery, Blandings Castle
        (Morning)
        Scene 2 – The exterior of Green Park Tube
        Station (midday)
        Scene 3 – The Morpheus Club, W.1.
        (afternoon)

Act II   The Oak Gallery, Blandings Castle (the
        following morning)

Act III A Keeper's Cottage, Blandings (the next
        morning)

the sparklers Aileen Peavey (Olive Blakeney) steals Lady Middlewick's ornaments when the light is out, and, feigning a swoon, passes them to Eddie Cootes (Aubrey Mather) Lord Middlewick (Clive Currie) is seen centre

Ab Eve Halliday the heroine Jane Baxter

Freddie Bosham (Reginald Gardiner) son of the Earl of Middlewick and Phyllis Jackson (Nonnie Taylor) fail to find the diamonds up the chimney

Rhododendrons for recognition Freddie Bosham (Reginald Gardiner) finds Psmith at the Underground lift, Green Street

Who's Who

20 September 1934 (19 performances)
Duke of York's Theatre, London

Producer: Lawrence Grossmith
Play: P.G. Wodehouse and Guy Bolton (based on
   PGW's novel, *If I Were You*)

Cast

Charles	ROLAND GILLETT
Slingsby	SEBASTIAN SMITH
Lady Lydia Bassinger	VIOLET VANBRUGH
The Hon. Freddie	LAWRENCE GROSSMITH
Chalk-Marshall	
Sir Herbert Bassinger	MORTON SELTEN
Tony, Earl of Droitwich	PETER HADDON
Ma Price	LAURA WRIGHT
Syd Price	IVOR BARNARD
Polly Brown	LILLIAN BOND
Violet Might	ENID STAMP TAYLOR
J.B. Might	CHARLES QUARTERMAINE

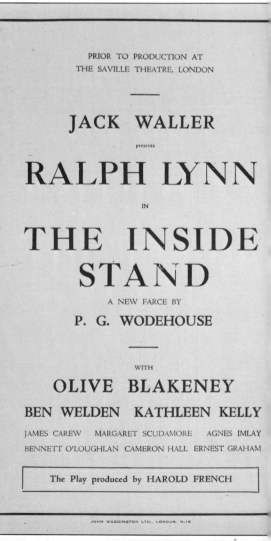

PRIOR TO PRODUCTION AT
THE SAVILLE THEATRE, LONDON

JACK WALLER

presents

RALPH LYNN

IN

THE INSIDE
STAND

A NEW FARCE BY
P. G. WODEHOUSE

WITH

OLIVE BLAKENEY

BEN WELDEN   KATHLEEN KELLY

JAMES CAREW   MARGARET SCUDAMORE   AGNES IMLAY
BENNETT O'LOUGHLAN   CAMERON HALL   ERNEST GRAHAM

The Play produced by HAROLD FRENCH

JOHN WADDINGTON LTD., LONDON. N.16

The Inside Stand

21 November 1935 (50 performances)
Saville Theatre, London

Producer: Jack Waller
Play: P.G. Wodehouse (based on his novel, *Hot Water*)
Director: Geoffrey Norman

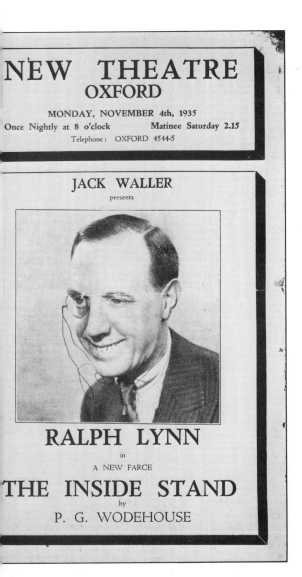

Cast

Sammy Simms	BEN WELDON
Duchess de la Vospierre	OLIVE BLAKENEY
Freddie Widgeon	RALPH LYNN
Miss Mossop	CLARE HARRIS
Parker	BENNETT O'LOGHLEN
Mr. Gedge	CAMERON HALL
Senator Fitch	JAMES CAREW
Josephine Fitch	KATHLEEN KELLY
Mrs. Gedge	ALETHA ORR

Act I Scene 1 – Corner of cocktail bar, Hotel
Splendide, St. Rocque
Scene 2 – Drawing room of Chateau Blissac
Act II Same
Act III Mrs. Gedge's boudoir

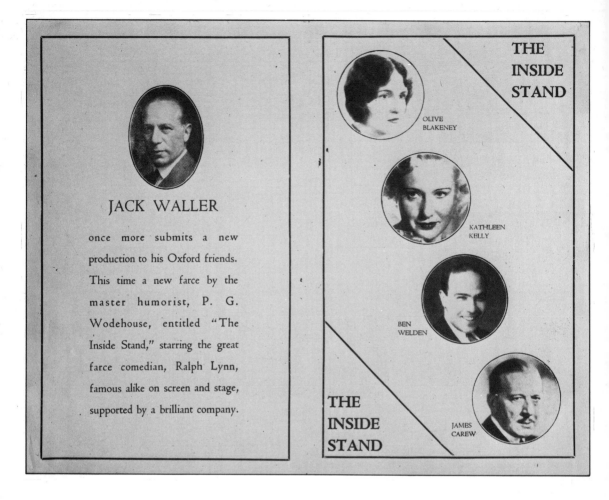

JACK WALLER

once more submits a new production to his Oxford friends. This time a new farce by the master humorist, P. G. Wodehouse, entitled "The Inside Stand," starring the great farce comedian, Ralph Lynn, famous alike on screen and stage, supported by a brilliant company.

OLIVE BLAKENEY

KATHLEEN KELLY

BEN WELDEN

JAMES CAREW

THE INSIDE STAND

THE INSIDE STAND

Don't Listen, Ladies

2 September 1948 (219 performances)
St. James's Theatre, London

Producers: Alec L. Rea and E.P. Clift
Play: P.G. Wodehouse (as Stephen Powys) and
    Guy Bolton (From the French of Sacha Guitry)
Director: William Armstrong

Cast

Daniel Bachelet, an antique dealer	FRANCIS LISTER
Henriette, a maid	PAMELA BEVAN
Madeleine, Daniel's second wife	CONSTANCE CUMMINGS
Baron De Charancay	D.A. MEHAN
Blandinet, Daniel's assistant	DENHOLM ELLIOTT
Julie Bille-en-Bois, an ex-actress	ADA REEVE
Valentine, Daniel's first wife	BETTY MARSDEN
A Porter	PETER FRANKLIN
Michel Aubrion	FERDY MAYNE

The action of the play passes in the room behind Daniel Bachelet's antique shop in the vicinity of the Place Vendome, Paris.

Act I   10:00 a.m. on a Monday in late spring
Act II   The following Friday afternoon
Act III The following Monday morning
           Time: The present

PGW used the pseudonym of Stephen Powys for this, his last play.

Next page: Constance Cummings and Francis Lister, stars of *Don't Listen, Ladies*.